Beads on a String

Peace, Joy, and Love

Compiled for WORDWRIGHTS

BARBARA SHEPHERD, Editor

Peace, Joy & Love
Always —
Jody Kass

Beads on a String – Peace, Joy, and Love
for Members of Wordwrights OKC Christian Writers
Barbara Shepherd, Editor

Published in the United States of America
by Art Affair
Post Office Box 54302
Oklahoma City, OK 73105

Cover art: Jody Karr "Peace, Joy, Love" (www.earthglowstudio.com)
Cover design: Barbara Shepherd (www.barbarashepherd.com)

First Printing December 2014
ISBN: 1503374262
ISBN-13: 978-1503374263

DEDICATION

Beads on a String – Peace, Joy, and Love is dedicated to all writers who write for Christian and secular markets, for family, or for the joy of writing. With Jesus Christ in their hearts, they are vessels to pour words on paper (or lighted screens) that convey His message of salvation, peace, and love.

ACKNOWLEDGEMENTS

Many Wordwrights members were introduced to the process of publication during the compilation of this anthology. Our "First Readers" read the majority of these pieces, noting their approval for theme and content; those comfortable with critiquing made suggestions for improvement and our editor provided deep edits. Participants revised their work, using their discretion, and resubmitted.

First Readers: Anita Breitling, Phyllis Dominguez, Diane Franke, Donna Le, Mona Jean Reed, Michele Simmons, Milton Smith, Connie Sorrell, Kathryn Spurgeon, Jean Stover, Norman Styers, Lori Williams, and Barbara Zimmerman.

Lori Williams was instrumental in accumulating bios from each of our participants. Barbara Zimmerman selected scriptures for fillers. Roz Reiff and Jody Karr assisted in proofing the book.

Twenty-five members of the Wordwrights OKC Christian Writers answered the call for manuscripts with more than seventy pieces chosen for publication.

Jody Karr created "Peace, Joy, Love," an original mixed media. She photographed it and graciously allowed her contemporary artwork to grace the cover of Beads on a String – Peace, Joy, and Love.

A special thanks goes to all mentioned above and to our editor, Barbara Shepherd, for her talent, dedication to detail, and hours of work donated in the creation of this book.

Beads on a String

Peace, Joy, and Love

Contents

Wordwrights OKC Christian Writers
presents:

Anita Breitling

Anita Breitling has been writing ever since she was old enough to read. As a seasoned citizen, she focuses her writing on science fiction and fantasy while also penning inspirational non-fiction. Find her devotional blog at www.anitabreitling.blogspot.com.

Knowing God through Our Dreams

I loved the days when the bookmobile came to town. It was like a little oasis in a small community. My children were in school, so I took my time going over the shelves in the van.

I wasn't looking for anything in particular, but when I saw a certain title, I grabbed the book off the shelf and thumbed through it. For years, I'd hoped to find something like this. I may have taken home other books that day, but I only remember this one.

Ever since I'd been in high school, I'd had a fascination with dreams and their meanings. I'd often go to the public library and search through titles for anything that could tell me about dreams. As a teenager, I skimmed through books that bordered on the occult and what's now termed *New Age*. I found nothing from a Christian perspective on dreams.

I gleaned some information from the few books that I'd read, but it wasn't until that day in the bookmobile that I found what I'd been seeking. It had taken me fifteen years to find the book by Herman Riffel: Your Dreams: God's Neglected Gift – Are You Missing God's Messages to You in Your Sleep?

It took me a short time to read for it was what I needed to start me back on the dream trail that I'd started at sixteen. I repented of reading all those secular books and asked the Lord to open my eyes to all He wanted me to know about dreams and interpretations.

I eventually bought my own copy of that book and reread it, underlining all the comments that caught my attention. I had started journaling my dreams as a teenager, but now journaling took on new meaning.

Another fifteen years went by and the information concerning dreams exploded! There were so many dream books on the market that I had a hard time deciding which to purchase. There were also dream ministries online, in churches, and workshops where people could be taught about their nighttime communications from God.

I have come to realize how important dreams are and how they have helped me sort out problems, given me warnings, shown me a bit of the future, and come as visions when I needed comfort or reassurance. As a writer, several dreams have been the catalyst for stories.

I recall with fondness the time I dreamt of a job that would be mine. A single parent at the time, I was comforted that work was available for me. I didn't know where or when, but the day I stood before the main frame of the telephone office, preparing to wire in phone numbers, I thought, *I've done this before*, and remembered that dream. It was a humbling experience.

I also remember the night vision I had the morning of my sister's death. In the dream, I saw four angels standing at the four corners of her hospital bed. A soft, green glow surrounded the room. Each angel took a corner of the bed sheet and lifted my sister up through the ceiling. I woke, knowing my sister had died. A few hours later, I received a call that she had indeed passed, and her time of death was within minutes of my vision.

I've been warned about storms coming in my life, and have received visions of loved ones in heaven. I've uncovered answers to prayers, reasons for spiritual unrest, and people or circumstances for whom I should pray.

I've even had a few dreams interpreted by a dream ministry and was amazed at how in-depth the meanings went. Our psyche is truly awesome, and only God can know the inner workings of a person's mind and emotions.

I don't journal my dreams as much now as I did when younger. I have matured enough in my walk with the Lord that I don't need the dreams interpreted as before. I do, however, write down those snippets that get my attention.

I'm thankful for learning about dreams and their meanings. Many of them have brought me peace of mind and an understanding of God who communicates through visions in the night. He loves me and wants me to know more of Him even while I sleep.

Anita Breitling

Smiley

(Based on a true story)

Smiley glanced again at his watch. Today, his parents were coming for a visit. His mom told him she'd made lasagna and brownies. His mouth watered just thinking about it. It was a blessing that the prison allowed families to bring in food. How much longer this privilege would last Smiley didn't know. He'd enjoy the meals as long as he could.

Now came his turn to enter the visitation room. First the routine search, then he hurried over to where his mom and dad waited. They embraced him.

"Do you want to eat first or visit?" His mom's dark eyes twinkled as she teased him.

"You know better than that. I'm more than ready for that lasagna." Smiley rubbed his hands together in anticipation. Pasta aroma surrounded the table where they sat.

Smiley's dad left to go get sodas while Smiley and his mom set out the meal.

"Dig in. Your dad's on his way back." Mom handed Smiley a paper plate. He dipped out a generous serving of the food.

"Hey, save some for the rest of us," Dad teased as he set down the cold drinks.

Smiley grinned, his mouth full of pasta.

In between bites, the trio shared bits and pieces of what had been going on in the month since they'd last seen each other.

Smiley sighed, patting his tummy. "Man, that's so go-o-o-d!"

"Ready for dessert?" Mom reached for the brownie container.

"Nah, let's wait a bit." Smiley wanted this visit to last as long as possible.

Dad handed some change to Smiley and asked if he would go get more soda. Smiley jumped up and quickly got the drinks. On the way back to the table, he noticed his parents talking earnestly between them. Immediately, he sensed something wasn't right.

"What's going on?" Smiley set the cans down and slipped back into his seat.

"Your mom has something to tell you." Dad leaned back and nodded to his wife.

With a deep sigh, Mom pushed her pink head scarf off her bald head, showing Smiley the three green dots marked there.

"The cancer's gone to my brain. The dots mark the place where the radiologist will put a mask on me during the radiation procedure." Mom's voice trembled with tears.

"Ah, man." Smiley reached around and gave his mom a hug, blinking back unshed tears. For several minutes, the three of them sat in silence.

"How 'bout those brownies?" Dad broke the intimate moment.

"Sure." Smiley released his mom and opened the container.

The rest of the visit flowed by in a blur. Smiley laughed and cut up with his mom, teasing her about her white hair growing back in and making her laugh at his silly jokes.

Later that evening Smiley lay on his bunk, arms behind his head, staring at the ceiling. His mom had cancer of the brain, a death sentence. Rolling over toward the wall, Smiley wept and prayed for his parents.

On a Monday evening shortly after that visit, Smiley headed to a worship service to hear John Banks preach.

Right in the middle of the service, John stopped and said, "Smiley, come here." Puzzled, Smiley walked to the front of the chapel.

"Lift your hands," John said. Smiley did and John laid his hands on Smiley's shoulders. "Smiley, I see God putting a large hedge of protection around you; keep hold of God because the enemy is coming to steal your smile."

Smiley returned to his seat, his mind churning. *What did that mean? Am I going to get beat up or robbed?* He set the negative thoughts aside and thanked God for His hedge of protection.

Approximately one month later, Smiley got word to go to the chapel. *Now what?* Leaving his work area where he sewed denim jeans, he proceeded to the chapel where he met Chaplain Don.

"You need to call home. I'll dial the number, Smiley, then hand you the phone." Don dialed a number, listened, and then handed the phone to Smiley.

Smiley listened to his sister, Grace, explain that their mom had been admitted to the hospital. Drugged with morphine, his mom was incoherent and unable to talk, but she could hear him if he wanted to tell her anything.

Smiley choked down a sob and then said, "Hi, Mom, I love you." He wanted to say more but couldn't get the words past the lump in his throat.

Grace came back on the line. "I'll get back with you later, brother. Please pray."

Smiley handed the phone back to the chaplain. Without a word, he headed to the sanctuary where he sat and prayed for his mom.

An hour later, Smiley trudged back to his unit. As he approached it, his case manager stopped him.

"Gotta take you to your cell, Smiley," Dewayne said.

Smiley entered his cell where Dewayne locked him down. Speaking through the glass window Dewayne said, "This is prison policy, Smiley. Your mom died, and you can't go to the funeral because we're understaffed."

Smiley sagged down onto his bunk; he sat there, numb. Suddenly, he saw a huge circle of demons standing before him and in the middle of that circle stood Jesus who held Smiley in a loving embrace. With his head lying on Jesus' chest, Smiley looked up and noticed the demons wearing banners proclaiming words like: guilt, sorrow, pain, oppression, and depression. Smiley looked back at Jesus and saw that His chest and eyes were burning like fire.

"Is that you, Lord?"

"Yes, it is, my son," the Lord said, "and I have you."

"Why does your chest burn?"

"It is the love I have for my children; it burns like fire."

"Why are your eyes burning?"

"I am watching the enemy. If they dare cross this hedge of protection that I have placed around you, I will cut them ASUNDER!" The last word rumbled like thunder.

Moments later, Dewayne returned and asked Smiley if he was okay. When Smiley answered yes, Dewayne released him from the cell saying, "The chaplain wants to see you again."

Smiley headed back to the chapel. Pausing a moment outside the chapel door, he glanced up. There, high in the sky, a large, white cloud floated, and right in its center shone a picture-perfect cross of blue sky. Smiley bowed his head and thanked the Lord for the vision and for this additional sign of His love.

Two weeks later, Smiley wondered at his seeming lack of grief concerning his mother's death. Deep inside, he heard these words: "Surely, I have borne all your grief and carried all your sorrow."

Smiley praised the Lord and then gave his mom a huge smile – the one the devil had tried to steal from him.

Anita Breitling

Wordwrights OKC Christian Writers
presents:

Rickey D. Briody

Rickey D. Briody lives in Edmond, Oklahoma, and enjoys writing short stories, poetry and devotionals. She received a bachelor's degree in English from Oklahoma State University and a master's degree in Speech Language Pathology from Lamar University in Beaumont, Texas. Rickey has had numerous articles published about special education law and practices. She has also had short stories published in popular magazines as well as in Oklahoma: The Fountain of the Heartland.

The Lavender Skirt

And now these three remain: faith, hope and love. But the greatest of these is love. (1 Corinthians 13:13 NIV)

I adored playing dress-up as a little girl. Mama gave me old jewelry, scarves, and articles of gently-used clothing that had the magical ability to transform my world. I often coveted one of her skirts or dresses, waiting for the day when she considered the garment worn sufficiently to be passed on to me. That's how it was with her lavender skirt.

Mama was royalty in that skirt, topping it off with a white cotton blouse. She had chestnut hair twisted into a stylish bun, and her hazel eyes were bright and intelligent. Although I was never the beauty that Mama was, I felt the skirt had the power to bring me close to Mama's level of pretty.

I never begged Mama for the skirt although my mouth watered when I saw her wear it. Begging would have been impolite and would not have made the waiting hurry along any faster. I had to be patient. I admired from afar knowing that someday it would be mine, shared with me in love.

The skirt was beautiful in its simplicity. Textured in a soft, supple weave, it was gathered at the waist by a conventional waistband. And its color! Too subtle to be called "purple," it reminded me of the lilacs growing on the big bush behind our house – a pretty, little girl color. Never mind that it had a worn spot here and there. It was exquisite. No price tag could come close to reflecting its value. Only Mama's love could do that.

As time passed, the lavender skirt with its washings and ironings eventually reached a point in its life where Mama considered it worthy of being my dress-up skirt. I finally had the privilege of slipping into its cotton coolness. It was heavenly and smelled like Mama. It felt like Mama. I was not only a great actress in that skirt; I was also a child clothed in love.

The lavender skirt was my magic carpet to transport me to the mysterious and allowed me to become – special, someone far from common. It took me to times and places beyond everyday imagination.

The skirt tumbled all the way down to my ankles as I wriggled into it. Mama fastened the waistband around me with a tiny, gold safety pin. I swished the cotton folds back and forth with my hands and twirled in humongous circles, feeling as if I had butterfly wings and could fly. That skirt had a freedom to it that let me become anything I dared to be.

On one occasion, I was a mother cuddling my newborn baby in the snow, trying to save my little one from the freezing cold. I wrapped the folds of the miraculous skirt around my baby doll as we trudged onward to an imaginary house in the distance. I was successful, of course. All because of the skirt.

Another time, I donned the skirt and became a famous singer, lilting out the only verse I knew of "Claire de Lune." Raising my hands to the sky, I sang, *I reach for, Clair de Lune As one obsessed, might reach for the moon...*

The skirt swept me away to a beach where haunting lyrics in the imaginary moonlight hung sweetly in the sea air. The ocean accompanied me with its rhythmic pounding, and the moon's reflection skittered across wave-enhancing white caps.

The best magic the skirt conjured transformed me into a blithe ballet dancer, floating around the living room which suddenly filled with billowing clouds. I danced the whirling dance of the dervish. I pranced like a proud prize pony. I performed pirouettes. My arms were beyond graceful, and I knew without a doubt I was the most elegant ballerina under God's glorious sun.

Throughout every adventure wearing the skirt, my Mama was there with her sweet smile. She was my ever patient, never complaining audience, cheering me on. Her applause was the finest encouragement a performer could hope for. And it took so little to earn it. Just to be there with her, weaving dreams with the wonderful lavender skirt.

When I close my eyes on a quiet afternoon in the spring or early summer and smell the perfume of the lilac bush, I am reminded of that whimsical skirt. I see Mama pinning me into it, sharing its beauty with me. I hear the applause and Mama telling me what a great performer I am.

Rickey D. Briody

Let's Make a Deal

Not long ago, I spent the day attending a children's writing conference for authors and wannabe authors of children's books. It was a great opportunity to meet many Oklahoma writers and listen to presenters speak about writing, publishing, illustrating, and so on. Much of it was motivational, to support us wannabes and give us encouragement to get on with it and get over the stage fright of this business.

At the end of the afternoon, door prizes were given by way of a drawing. Prizes included books donated by various authors attending the conference. Each participant had a folder for notes and handouts. The folder had a numbered ticket stapled inside for the drawing.

I sat staring at those numbers and thought, "Okay, God, if you really want me to get serious about writing that book, please let me win a door prize." Then, feeling a bit of shame and guilt, I backtracked. "Okay, God, I know I'm not supposed to make bargains with you. So, forget it. That was selfish of me." I waffled. I pushed the guilt aside. I gulped. Internally, I whispered, "But, God, it sure would be a sign from you if I won a door prize. It would let me know that you want me to write that book." Sounded rather childish even to me.

The event hostess drew the first number from the basket. Slowly and deliberately, she read the five-digit number aloud. I followed along in my folder, touching each number in unison with her boldly projected voice. My digits magically corresponded to the sequence of those announced. I sat there, staring at the folder in disbelief. The hostess called the number a second time. Sure enough, that was my number.

I claimed my prize with a Cheshire-cat grin on my face. I won a children's chapter book written by a talented Oklahoma author who graciously signed the book for me.

Now I had done it. I had held a conversation with the omniscient One. Made a Promise. I wonder if I'll be held to it? I wonder how long I have to make good on the deal. Guess I'd better get busy and write a few lines.

Rickey D. Briody

Beads to inspire:

Peace

You will keep him in perfect peace, whose mind is stayed on You, because he trusts in You. Trust in the Lord forever, for in Yah, the Lord, is everlasting strength.

(Isaiah 26:3,4 NKJV)

Wordwrights OKC Christian Writers
presents:

Misti Chancellor

Misti Chancellor currently serves as Wordwrights' newsletter editor. Her other writing activities involve serving in an advisory capacity to the young people in her church as they compile and publish their church newsletter, writing technical documents in her role as a business analyst on her job, and occasionally updating her blog: (http://scribblesandmusings.wordpress.com/). She may be contacted through her blog or at mlchancellor@hotmail.com.

Count It All Joy

"My brethren, count it all joy when ye fall into divers temptations; Knowing this, that the trying of your faith worketh patience." (James 1:2-3)

I can't say the layoff came as a total surprise, not when I'd been praying that God would allow me to keep my job until I found something else. I knew the state of my finances, and I knew that I couldn't financially survive a layoff as things were. I'd been looking for another job. I'd even put in applications at several places and been through one HR screen phone call already. I knew I could find another job, if things would just settle until I could. The day after I prayed that prayer, I was laid off right after returning from lunch.

It's hard to describe what that feels like to someone who hasn't been there. There's a whole gamut of emotions you go through. Helplessness. Feeling sick. Shock, mostly. The one feeling I remember after the initial shock was unexplainable peace. Before I ever reached home, I received a call from a recruiter, who had been made aware of the situation by my manager (who had been laid off a few days before.) By the time I arrived home, I had two different positions to apply for. (Good managers care about their people. This manager was exceptional.) That was the beginning of a whirlwind of applications and interviews.

My biggest fear was losing my house. I had enough money to get through the first month, but I didn't know how I was going to manage after that. An anonymous donation, made through the church, covered my house payment for the next month.

Then tragedy struck. On May 20, 2013, an EF5 tornado roared through my hometown, created a terrible mess, and took several lives. My brother's family lost their home (thankfully, they were spared and escaped with only bruises and scrapes.) My church was damaged. Life became chaotic, but God showed us that even tragedies can work for our good.

I moved to my parents' home, and my brother and his family lived in my home and paid my bills while they were settling the situation with their insurance company and finding a new home.

The worry about losing my home was handled. I didn't have a job yet and didn't know how long it would take to find one, but the financial burden was lifted. Unemployment payments covered the bills that my brother wasn't paying. My brother's family had a place to stay together comfortably and could work things out without feeling pressured into doing something right away. They had all the furniture and necessities to live without having to go and purchase all that immediately. God took both tragedies and worked to help us help each other.

The day after the tornado, I had a job interview for a position that I had applied for three weeks prior to being laid off. Damage from the tornado and all the traffic complications from people who wanted to see the devastation made it impossible to know how long it would take to get to the interview. Arriving in the area early gave me the opportunity to visit with friends who worked down the block from the interview site and set my nerves at ease. The interview went well.

After the interview, I made my way back to my hometown. I went to see where I could help with cleanup. Because of the damage and snarled traffic, it was easier to haul a bicycle with you, park where you had to, and ride from there during the first week after the tornado. I had my bike in my vehicle, and so I parked, changed to tennis shoes, and rode off. First stop was my church.

The fellowship hall was completely destroyed. The church building was also hit. Several congregants were at the building to salvage what we could. A few hours later, I climbed back on my bike and rode the half mile to my aunt's house to check on her, my uncle and my grandma who was in frail health. At the end of the day, I made my way back to my car, loaded my bike, and was able to drive home. They had just reopened the street in front of the church.

The next few weeks were spent focusing on tornado cleanup, with a few job interviews here and there. Tragedy has a way of refocusing priorities. I might not have had a job, but at least I had food, shelter, and family nearby who were safe. My needs were provided for. I couldn't offer things or money to those in need, but I did have time and energy, and those were needed, too.

As that situation stabilized, it became apparent that my sister in Idaho could use some help as she entered the last few weeks before her first baby came. She was having some difficulties and her husband wasn't able to take off at that time to help her. Naturally, my mom wanted to go and Dad wasn't able to leave just yet, due to his obligations as the pastor related to the tornado situation and a contract he had to finish before he could fully retire.

As we were trying to figure out how I could take her but still look for a job, an answer came in the form of a job offer from the place I had interviewed the day after the tornado. I was able to accept the offer and set a start date that would allow me to take my mom to my sister's and stay with them until my dad was able to join them. We left for Idaho the next morning.

Ten weeks after being laid off, I was able to start my new job. My nephew joined the family, happy and healthy. My brother and his family found a beautiful new home, and I was able to return to mine. Approximately nine months after the tornado, my church family was able to move back into our building.

You learn a lot when you go through tragic or traumatic events. If you're watching, you see God move to bring about good from things that feel so horrible and terrible when they happen. You see the goodness of humanity, the drive to help others, to give selflessly for their needs. You find blessings in the trouble, and faith grows. In the middle of the storm, you find peace. In the aftermath, you find love. In recovery, you find joy.

Misti Chancellor

Beads to inspire:

Joy

When they saw the star, they rejoiced with exceedingly great joy.

(Matthew 2:10 NKJV)

Wordwrights OKC Christian Writers
presents:

Barbara Culbertson

Barbara Culbertson has written devotionals for her denomination's mission magazine and curriculum for a course in developmental psychology. She has a BS and an MEd in education and an MS in counseling psychology. She delights in sharing stories about people who have influenced her, especially in countries where she has served as a missionary with her husband. She enjoys their seven grandchildren and traveling, especially on mission trips. Barbara has a private counseling practice in Oklahoma City and teaches online. She can be reached at barb_j_c@juno.com.

Dwelling

We were well into the middle of our third furlough, that one-year-in-five spent in our "home" country, after four years as overseas missionaries. The year had been especially meaningful, communicating with U.S. churches how the Lord was working in Haiti. I told about going to bed hearing Haitians' prayers resounding through the mountains surrounding our campus, praying for an end to what seemed to be imminent civil war. When the dictator was whisked out of the country with very little bloodshed, you couldn't convince those Haitian Christians that wasn't a direct answer to their impassioned pleas! We shared Madame Jean's testimony to God's goodness even after all her belongings had been stolen on a cross-country bus trip. I relived the wonder of Marie-Marte extending grace to raise the son her husband had fathered with a prostitute, after the child's mother died. What joy to share how Haitian Christians experience and testify to God's goodness in the midst of unfathomable hardship.

Furlough allowed my children to experience the U.S. culture I'd grown up in. I enjoyed hours stocking up on taco shells and little girls' dresses, in assorted sizes to last the next four years. Those K-Mart "Blue Light Specials" were especially fun. But inside, I was feeling what our five-year-old had questioned getting ready for that first furlough 15 years earlier. In my mind, I relived that conversation, remembering joyfully exclaiming, "We're going home!"

Matthew had contested, "But, Mommy, we *are* home! *This* – *this* is home!"

Our family had arrived in Europe when he was a year old, and Italy was all he recognized as "home." He loved to peruse the *giocatolerie* we passed on the way to school each day, with their myriad of tempting toys. He had never entered a Toys-R-Us, and I couldn't wait to take his hand and stroll those aisles with, not scores, but thousands of delights! Yet, I realized he was right; this was indeed "home." Still, like the "visions of sugarplums" that danced in the children's heads in Clement Moore's classic, *A Visit from St. Nicholas,* my mind entertained visions of malted milk balls, marshmallows, pumpkin pies and Thanksgiving. I looked forward to ordering a meal in a restaurant and actually getting what I'd intended to order – ruefully remembering the waiter's startled face when I confused *melanzana* with *zanzare* and mistakenly ordered pizza with mosquitoes rather than eggplant.

I brought my mind back to the present. In the midst of packing accumulated supplies, of watching for sales on all the stuff I wanted to stock up on, that "Blue Light Special" suddenly got stuck in the "on" mode. My husband had agreed to remain one more year as "missionary in residence" at the university where he was teaching.

During this "one more year," I immersed myself in an in-depth Bible study and other activities. Still, most days I'd rather have been "home" either Haiti, or Italy, or . . . (fill in the blank). Oh well, I told myself, I could handle McDonald's and Penn Square Mall one more year.

God sent me a precious lady who became my mentor. She taught me to dig into the Word in ways I'd never experienced. One passage we explored was Ps. 37, "Do not fret. . ." (vs. 1).

Was I fretting? I wasn't even sure I knew what that was. Our culture doesn't talk much about "fretting." But as I sought to excuse and rationalize my attitude, God kept coming back to this word. I finally had to admit I was fretting.

My attitude needed to change. But how? The Psalm continues, "Trust in the Lord and do good; dwell in the land and enjoy safe pasture" (37:3, NIV). That "enjoy" sounded good, albeit hard to attain. Seemed like a key might be in the "dwelling." No wonder my attitude wasn't working.

As the second year of furlough came to a close, I looked forward to making airline reservations and finally getting "home." Then the nightmare became reality. My husband was again asked to remain teaching "one more year." The "Blue Light Special" really *was* stuck! I tried to explain my feelings, but people just didn't understand. After all, hadn't God called me to overseas missionary service? Nevertheless, as I prayed along with my husband, we agreed that God was indeed telling us to remain where we were.

Still, I ached for the overstuffed Tap-Taps to transport us to church over those foot-deep pot-holes. I missed shopping in the shadow of Brunelleschi's Duomo, strolling over the Ponte

Vecchio, recalling how its riches were miraculously saved during WWII, and its art treasures restored after the 1966 Arno flood. Sweltering summer days brought longing for a refreshing shower in the spectacular cascades of Haiti's Saut-d'Eau waterfall.

But what if "dwelling" didn't indicate just a location? The U.S. surely had marvels of its own. Certainly the "home" I longed for had to do with people as well, like Gianni and Mariella, who gave up their homeland to study to become the pastors God had called them to be. Like Fausta, who called our church "her" church even though she hadn't as yet become a believer. Like Cristina, who gave up imaginings of becoming a "lady of Milan," woman of the world, to respond to God's call to holy living. Like Rocio, who discovered a God who embraces when others abandon.

Yet, as God continued to work in my heart and life, I realized my cross-cultural friendships weren't the total answer either. God had also given me relationships in the U.S. – reconnecting with a friend after 40 years, making friends with Leah who listened and cared more deeply than I could have imagined possible, and meeting David, who shared the excitement of phoning his mother to communicate that he'd returned to the church and life-style in Christ that she had instilled.

My struggle led me to Jeremiah 17:7-8 (NIV): "Blessed is the one who trusts in the Lord, whose confidence is in him. They will be like a tree planted by the water that sends out its roots by the stream. It does not fear when heat comes . . . It has no worries in a year of drought and never fails to bear fruit."

That first "one more year" did seem like a year of drought. Yet, it led me to the stream that produces fruit. It's been 25 "one more years." I have continued to struggle, and some days I'd rather be in Italy, or Haiti, or Ecuador. But I have learned that "dwelling" is not the place, or even the people, although it certainly has to do with relationship. As Psalm 37 emphasizes, if I want to enjoy safe pastures I must *dwell*. My mentor during those early years directed me to Hannah Hurnard's *Hinds' Feet on High Places,* based on Hab. 3:19: "He makes my feet like hinds' feet and will make me to walk [not to stand still in terror, but to walk] and make [spiritual] progress upon my high places [of trouble, suffering, or responsibility]!" (Amp).

Dwelling is not found in Blue Light Specials or even a specific location. The spiritual progress it brings comes in high places, at times with trouble and suffering and responsibility. It results in the enjoyment and safe pasture of Psalm 37:3.

Barbara Culbertson

The Tree

We have two. Christmas trees, that is. It started when our daughter came home from college late in December. We had already put up our tree, but she still wanted to decorate. Solution? Two trees – artificial and real. Twenty years later, we continue our "extra tree" tradition that ushers in the Advent season.

When my husband and I found ourselves 2700 miles from home just after Thanksgiving, my mind naturally fast-forwarded to Christmas in Oklahoma. Our four-month Spanish course was over; it was time to pack suitcases.

As I walked the half-mile down the steep hill into our suburb of Carcelen for the last time, the Christmas trinkets that lined the streets tempted me. Vendors gestured and called in limited English, trying to lure this obvious Gringo. Their wares enticed – a small Nativity set of *mazipan* bread dough would lend a distinctive Ecuadorian flavor to our house. Or an elaborately embroidered table cloth, in the native Kechwa style. No, my suitcase was already pushing the 50-pound limit.

I thought about our Spanish teacher, Magdala, as I trudged back up the hill. How I looked forward to her supper invitation that last night in Quito! I remembered when I had first met her.

"At least I did not witness my mother's death like my sisters who were in that car crash with her," Magdala had recounted. "My parents occasionally took me to church. When my mother died when I was 12, I believed no one cared. My father grew more and more distant, and I grew angry with God. By the time I entered university, I felt isolated and alone. I rarely attended church; I especially disliked Christmas, with its emphasis on happy family times.

"I earned a graduate degree, traveled, and gained experience as a language teacher, including a job in an embassy. I tried to fill the void in my life with a boyfriend, and one night our passions took over, and. . . ." She hesitated, struggling as she revealed her pain, then continued, "I became pregnant. I was horrified; this did not portray the values I thought I embraced. God felt further distant as I dealt with the reality that my boyfriend decided to not be an active part of our son's life." Magdala stopped there; further details had to wait for another time.

I learned later that Magdala had encountered a committed Christian who took her to doctor's appointments and talked to her about a God who cares. Magdala's life began to change as she sought to fill the emptiness she'd felt so long. She talked about putting in many "knee" hours praying. Despite the language barrier, we became what Anne of Green Gables calls "kindred spirits" as we prayed for each other and shared spiritual struggles.

Now my thoughts were interrupted as my husband and I clambered on board the jam-packed trolley, vying for a seat on our hour-long bus ride across Quito to meet Magdala and her son by the artisan market. Noting my cane, a gentleman kindly gave me his place. As I sat down, I was startled to realize the indigenous woman beside me was caressing the chicken on her lap. She explained it was her pet, then offered me a further treat by inviting me to pet it! Soon another Kechwa woman boarded, with her ornately embroidered blouse, shawl, and long skirt, her baby strapped on her back. Although we jostled along rocky roads, that baby remained secure! And an additional bonus – a free back massage from elbows as we tried to make room for "just one more."

Merchants crowded on, laden with massive loads of oranges, carved wooden souvenirs, and vegetables on their backs. Vendors boarded the buses at the front and hawked their wares – candy, fruit, and toys--then made their way to the back, exited, and waited for the next bus. Entertainers waited at the stop lights – fire eaters, jugglers, mimes – vying to eke out a living by offering a bit of diversion to the travelers.

About half the bus seemed to recognize our U.S. accent and wanted to help us find the right stop, seeing a chance to practice their English. We managed to stumble off the bus and make our way to where Magdala and her son Pablo were waiting. Taxis whizzed past, and we decided to just hike the mile to her house, relishing sights and sounds of Quito for a last time. As we passed more vendors with Christmas ware, I wondered about Magdala's house—would she have decorated for Christmas, or was her hurt still too raw?

The small homey apartment, although only 10 miles from the equator, was chilly at 9500 feet. I admired her décor, a reflection of her travels. But there was little to remind one that Christmas was getting close.

Then I saw it. Magdala followed me to the corner where their three-foot Christmas tree stood with its few brightly painted glass ornaments. Her dialogue picked up where her story had left off previously.

"For years I rejected having a Christmas tree," she explained. "Even after I found a personal, committed relationship with God, I couldn't cope with Christmas and its association of families and traditions. I wanted to celebrate Jesus' birth with my son, but somehow a tree reminded me of the God who had left me without a mother at a vulnerable age. It reminded me of abandonment. My little boy was growing up without an earthly father who cared. No, I decided – no tree at Christmas."

"But you have one," I countered. "What changed?"

"A friend confronted me," Magdala explained. "She posed some hard questions. Was it OK for bitterness to overshadow the meaning of Christmas? A meaning that is symbolized, in part, by a tree? Was it OK for my little boy to grow up without the symbol of a Christmas tree, a symbol that would allow us to talk about grace, forgiveness, acceptance, and a Father who does not abandon His children?

"I then recognized how deep my anger toward God had been. As I confessed this, I acknowledged that God's forgiveness needed to be symbolized in a Christmas tree. So, five years ago, I put up my first Christmas tree."

I had difficulty not tearing up as Magdala and I embraced. A three-foot Christmas tree beside us symbolized what bound us together—different nationalities, different languages, but a Savior who chose to be a part of *our* world. My Ecuadorian Christmas souvenir was now burned into my heart.

The next evening my husband and I boarded a plane to return to the U.S. Two days later we began unpacking the 90 boxes of Christmas decorations. We put up the two trees. As I placed each of the ornaments – gifts from friends, memories of places – I still pictured Magdala's petite tree.

That last night in Quito was a high point of our four-month stay in Ecuador. My trees continue to remind me of a three-foot tree in Ecuador that represents a God who connects with people, a

God who does not abandon. A small Christmas tree will forever remain in my mental photo album to remind me that our God came to earth, became one of us, and restores relationship with Him and therefore with others, even in other countries and languages.

Barbara Culbertson

Wordwrights OKC Christian Writers
presents:

Phyllis Dominguez

Phyllis Dominguez is blessed to play French horn, for over 50 years now, and delights in horn-kazoo duos with her oldest granddaughter. The youngest keeps a good tempo on the rattle. Maracas anyone?

Thanks to the girls, Phyllis gets to read wonderful illustrated stories said to be for children – out loud – especially Dr. Seuss out loud. She also enjoys detective fiction, newspapers, history, P. G. Wodehouse, cartoon strips, vintage Looney Tunes – and music. Phyllis lives in Oklahoma City with her husband and practices futile diplomacy between a Jack Russell terrier and an audacious housecat. For all this, for country, church, family, friends, poets and inspirational writers, she is grateful.

Sing Choirs of Angels

"Help me!" Mother cried. Hardly anyone paid any mind as we moved through the lobby. The nurse behind the main desk looked up and smiled; one of the circle of TV-watchers glanced away from the flickering screen. The whole place smelled like floor wash. Not a bad facility, but somehow even the Christmas decorations along the walls made it seem more bleak.

"I don't know what to do!" Mother had shouted and pleaded since I'd arrived, the same few phrases over and over. It made for painful listening.

As her dementia advanced, a doctor had explained, it caused an electrical disturbance in her brain. Her anxiety and agitation were like the flash and sputter of a damaged electrical cord, her frightened repetitions like sparks. Tranquilizing drugs would subdue the short circuit and free her from the fear. And they did work, when she could take them.

But Mother had been ill and hospitalized. Doctors there discontinued the tranquilizers to safeguard her life, then declared her well enough to return to the nursing home, but without ordering her prescription for tranquilizers restored. Staff confirmed she was sleeping badly and constantly cried out – at night too. Yes, doctors had been informed; the prescriptions would come. In the meantime, Christmas arrived.

No matter what difficulties lodged between my mother and me over the years, Christmas had been a truce day, a day of gifts and smiles that persisted even after her dementia swept all other recollection away. Last year, she had relished her Christmas stocking, reached deep inside, pulled out her fruit and little treats, put them back, pulled them out again with brand-new surprise, put them back, pulled them out, all of us pleased.

This year, nursing center staff advised against bringing her home. On Christmas Eve, my sister and her husband had tried, only to have Mother shout and plead among their guests until everyone was suffering. My sister had to bring her back.

What could my own family do but endure Mother's distress? She was too upset this year even for Christmas stockings, and experience had taught me that within seconds of stepping out our front door, she would forget ever arriving.

And so I came tonight. Christmas night.

"Help me!" she said, "What am I going to do?"

"We're going to look at the lights." Celebrations might be over, but many people hadn't turned off their outdoor decorations. Mother liked to ride in the car. And – many years ago, when we were all young, she had made outings to see Christmas lights a family tradition. I hoped these pleasures might connect somehow in her brain to quiet the storm. They might help me, too. I found her shoes, buttoned her into a warm jacket, and led her to the car.

"Help me," she said as we drove off. "Somebody help me!"

Heaven help us both. If I broke any traffic laws. . . I could see us stopped, with Mother yelling out for help just as a young burly policeman strolled up to my car window. We headed for the first neighborhood lights available.

Thank you, God, for a radio station playing carols. Even with years of performing in band and singing in church choir, I still loved the old Christmas songs and cranked up the volume.

Mother shouted louder. "Help! Help me! Somebody...."

Okay, okay. . . I dialed down the music, and she got softer.

"Look at the lights." I pointed. "Aren't they beautiful? Look, those are all blue, wrapped around the tree."

"Ooh." For a few seconds she fell silent, soothed – maybe – by the tiny sparks of color shining through the darkness. This might work.

"What am I going to do?" she said.

"Look, look at the lights. See there?"

"Ooh...."

I had a quick grateful thought of hands that hauled ladders, put up hooks, separated yards of tangled cords, and braved bitter winds. *God bless Christmas lights....*

"Help me!"

And so it went, over and over. At least the music was there – the carols. Mother didn't seem to notice them, but they kept me going, up and down one street, then another. I worked to keep her eyes on the lights; the old songs continued, and slowly her cries grew slightly further apart.

But it wasn't enough. I'd have to drive all night at this rate. Every time she cried out, some inner part of me jerked. Each time I felt pity and frustration, and each time I felt more and more like brittle glass.

Then we drove down another sparkling street, and it happened.

"O Come All Ye Faithful" played from the radio, sung by a choir. Mother fell silent. Absolutely silent.

Why? I glanced away from my driving, trying to see her face in the dark car. Was it the song? Why that one and not the others?

Could be simple exhaustion. I knew about that. I tried not thinking about it until the singing ended.

"I don't know what to do!" she said.

"I don't either." Reaching over, I touched her hand. "Look there. See the pretty lights?"

The nursing home was quiet when we returned, one aide on duty at the desk, the corridor lights dimmed.

"Somebody help me!" Mother let me tug the nightgown over her head. "What am I going to do?" She lay down on her bed and I covered her with the blankets.

"Don't leave me here!" She grabbed my arm, a desperate grip.

"I'll be back." I got my arm free. Tears pricked my eyes. I wanted to gather her up, to carry her away from this place, away from all her fears. "I've got to wash my hands." I tried to keep my voice easy.

"Help me," she said.

I remembered the carol on the car radio. "O come all ye faithful..." I sang. Strange how difficult that was to do, alone in this stark little room. I tried to keep my voice soft, but it seemed to echo clear out to the hallway. "Joyful and triumphant...."

"O come ye, O come ye to..." I gathered up her clothes and put them in the hamper. She was quiet, I realized, just as she had quietened in the car. What was it with this song?

"...Born the King of angels..." What was it with music? I had played and sung most of my life, and I still didn't know what it was. "O come let us adore Him, O come let us..." People gave you definitions, but they all fell short.

Two verses of the lyrics I knew, and might cobble together three.

"...Sing, choirs of angels..." I walked into the tiny bathroom, washed my hands, and came out again.

"...Glory to God, glory in the highest..." Mother hadn't spoken for some time. I kept singing, softer, and moved closer to her bed.

She was asleep. In the space of two verses of that carol, with no tranquilizers and no sleeping pills. I finished my chorus and waited, marveling.

She didn't stir.

Thank you, God. I snapped off the light and stood listening outside her door. Blessed silence, blessed sleep, delivered in a song about choirs of angels. For me, this moment was Peace on Earth.

Later, nursing staff said she slept through the whole night.

Phyllis Dominguez

Stable

Why had I promised?

Because my sister had asked me in November. Christmas seemed a long way off in November, and I like horses. She kept two in town, I got to ride now and then, and she would be away this Christmas. Could I feed them once or twice over the holiday?

Today, on Christmas Eve, I still liked horses. But with dusk falling, the November promise tasted bitter in my mouth. The day had passed in a blur, marathon cleaning, presents not wrapped, last-minute obligations, and probably no sleep tonight. This was all done in love, but sometimes Christmas never quite came for me. Afterward, I'd find myself anticipating the day as if it hadn't already passed by while I was busy and exhausted.

But horses need feed. I had given my word, and I knew them by name – Sugar and Smokey. White and black, they nickered and ambled out of the shadows at the sound of my car door and the gate chain. Their peaceful exhaling made streamers of pale vapor in the graying light. The pasture sat well back from a semi-rural city street, trees, brush and scattered houses, concealing it from casual traffic.

I dragged the gate shut and felt a quick chill of isolation, but looked again at the horses. Easy swaying necks, relaxed ears, not too pricked, not laid back. They were thinking food, not fear, and their calm made it unlikely that some human danger lurked here – hidden to me maybe, but not to them. And there could be no haste in the pasture either. No sudden movements that spooked horses, no matter how fast I needed to get this done.

Sugar and Smokey loomed close in the fading sunset, then fell in a couple of feet behind me, their hooves thudding on the grass before striking slow and solid on the hard-trodden path to the horse shed. The little building was an informal affair, weathered, gap-planked here and there, but the roof didn't leak.

Through the wide door, I sidestepped the horses, and once inside, breathed in a sudden and strong, earthy fragrance: thick straw, alfalfa hay, grain and much more – the ancient odor of stables. For the first time in the whole day, the clamor in my brain stopped. I remembered what *day* was here. Here with me in a stable, at evening, surrounded by the honest smells of friendly animals.

I scooped grain from a barrel and thought about Mary and her baby, with Joseph, shoulder to withers in a place like this. The horses chomped at the feed with contented switches of their tails. I watched, made sure the barrels were secured, and looked about for other small tasks. But it was time to leave.

Stepping outside to face west, I saw the December evening star, brilliant in the clarity of a blue-dark Oklahoma sky, above a horizon rimmed with translucent layers of red and gold.

Thank you, God, for that November promise.

Nothing had changed about the night to come. The packages still needed wrapping. There would be little sleep. But this year, I would not miss Christmas.

I had been to the stable.

Phyllis Dominguez

Wordwrights OKC Christian Writers
presents:

Diane Alexander Franke

Diane Franke volunteers in the Ministry of Prayer and lends a hand with the senior citizens' meals at the Methodist Church. She writes poems and spiritual short stories based on a life lived in faith with the teachings of the Holy Spirit. She can be reached at difranke@swbell.net.

Anointed

Sparks of light, held prisoner in hot coals, waited to explode. Red and orange flames danced in the night. Smells from cooking food mixed with odors from nearby animals.

A man in hood and cloak stepped from the shadows of trees. He looked at the people waiting around their campfires. Their Storyteller had arrived.

Leaning on his staff, he shouted out, "Hear the story about a man, both human and divine."

"By act of baptism, a spiritual union between a Father and His son, caused a Divine Spirit to wind Its Light and Presence around the heart of mankind and change the world forever."

"Tonight, you will hear of a man who lived, worked, and walked among us. He laughed as we do. He hurt. He cried. He loved his family. Of lowly birth, he was anointed by God in a ceremony to become the Savior who would lead his people into a new world. He is Jesus, the man from Nazareth. Now begins this story."

Jesus watched the dew sparkle in the rising sun.

Bird song filled the air. Laughing, Jesus whistled a few notes and tossed bread crumbs out the window. "What a beautiful day," Jesus said, his heart full of joy. A smile lifted the corners of his mouth. Today, he needed to understand what was happening to him. He needed His Father's counsel. Pulling on a cloak, the son of a carpenter left home. His muscular legs, strong from lifting heavy loads of wood and stone, carried him into the countryside. Stopping a moment to feel the wind on his face and inhale fresh air, he turned and said, "I will always remember from whence I came."

Familiar with his surroundings, he walked over to a place under the trees and sat down. His soft eyes looked into the distance, then closed as he covered his head in prayer and said, "Father, I seek your counsel to begin to do Your Will."

His Father answered him. Later, Jesus uncovered his head in gratitude and walked home in peace.

He stopped for a moment to listen to a friend's troubles. As Jesus smiled into tired eyes, the villager's burdens felt lighter.

Walking on, Jesus opened his family's garden gate and started picking herbs and vegetables. A strong-faced woman smiled from a window and told her son that his meal was ready.

Everyone worked at home. His sisters cooked, sewed and weaved. His brothers tilled the soil and worked alongside Jesus in Joseph's carpenter shop. It was a busy, happy home.

In the evenings, Jesus told stories about their people, the Jews, and their history. He spoke of prophets and what happened to their nation when laws and covenants with God were broken.

Sometimes, he would tell them stories about their father, Joseph, who had died in an accident. Ancient Jewish custom dictated that Jesus as the oldest male child had the responsibility to provide for his mother, Mary, and his brothers and sisters.

He was tired tonight. Friends had visited, and it was late before they left. After walking his guests to the door, he looked up at a majestic sky, filled with stars that stretched far and wide, pouring their light over humanity.

"Father," he sighed, reveling in their design, "thank you for such beauty."

He lay on his bed and quickly fell asleep. Mary walked to the side of his bed, bent down, and kissed his brow. She touched his hands, tucked in his covers and whispered, "I love you."

Jesus stirred and a peaceful smile passed over his face.

Early the next morning, Jesus rolled out of bed and combed his hair with a calloused hand. He rubbed grit out of his eyes and washed his face.

He sat at the breakfast table and quietly ate. After his meal, he firmly wrapped his cloak around his shoulders and waist.

"Mother," he said, looking into Mary's eyes. He held her hands. "I am going to be baptized. I am not sure when I will return."

Anxious, Mary held him close, tears filling her eyes. He turned to his brother James and asked him to take care of their mother and family while he was gone. Jesus knew it would be some time before he returned to his mother's home.

Nodding goodbye, he left their house.

It will take three days to walk to my cousin John's camp, he thought to himself.

At noon, he ate unleavened bread and fed his thirst at a small brook. While he rested, his eyes swept across the fertile land, filled with colorful plants and flowers. He saw lambs playing while rams grazed next to ewes.

On he trod, stopping occasionally to shake a pebble from his sandals or slap at a wandering insect. Resting at night, he covered himself with his cloak.

Soon . . . tomorrow, he thought as he drifted into sleep.

The day of his baptism commenced with a stirring in the air. An early riser, Jesus was walking down the road with a fellow traveler when he was startled by the cry of an eagle floating high above him. Its shadow briefly crossed his face. Looking around, he saw the river just ahead and waved goodbye to his companion.

As he joined the crowd at the Jordan River waiting to be baptized, he thought, *There will be no time to visit with John.*

Jesus was somber as he stepped into the Jordan's cold water. Goose bumps popped up on his arms and legs. Time held its breath.

The air was thick with expectancy. John leaned forward and questioned, "Why? It is I who should be baptized by you."

"Suffer it to be so now: for thus it becometh us to fulfill all righteousness. It is proper for us to do this," Jesus said.

The son of man bowed his head in prayer and submission and slipped into the water. John spoke, and the words raced throughout heaven.

Thunderous music sounded across the universe while celestial lightning tore open heaven's gate. Realms of angels worshipped and sang. The Father's Spirit descended in the form of a dove. Lighting upon Him, God spoke. "This is my beloved Son in whom I am well pleased."

Clouds of heavenly light shimmered and God poured all authority and power upon His Son.

Jesus, praying and filled with the Presence of God, stood up in the river. Drops of water fell like rain from his body, shimmering and dancing in the sunlight. Baptized with truth, he stepped forward and took his anointed place.

Transfixed, John wept, his eyes filled with questions. "Is Jesus Israel's Messiah and Savior?"

"I am," Jesus said, looking into John's searching eyes.

Jesus Christ, anointed by God during his baptism, was now the Light of the World. Full of the Holy Spirit, he took his cloak and left the Jordan River. His face confident, He was led by the Spirit into the desert wilderness for a time of testing.

Finished speaking, the storyteller lifted his staff and walked off into the morning light.

Diane Alexander Franke

A Trip Home

Have you ever been bitten by a cat that thinks you are the canary and he's not going to let go? It leaves an everlasting impression, and in my case, a scar. This happened in my late twenties, on one of my trips to visit my parents in southeastern Oklahoma. They lived in the country on forty acres that smelled like warm meadows and green, moist moss. Their home was surrounded by fragrant oak and pine trees. Dogwood and redbud trees grew close to the creek down the hill and burst into flowery life every spring.

I am the third generation of my family to own this land. One hundred years ago, my grandfather planted cotton and peanuts in the sandy loam. He would tie his mules to the sapling trees on top of the hill after working the land. He would lean into the traces towards his mule as he plowed. He curved his furrows to prevent soil from washing downhill when the spring rains came before the seeds had sprouted and rooted enough to hold the rich dirt together. When I visit, I see the rows he worked. Blue stem and Bermuda grass now grow there. Sometimes I lie down on the ground just to smell the soil and gaze up through a green canopy of leaves covering tall oak and hickory trees and listen to the wind soughing through the pine trees.

On this day, my husband Richard and I drove up the crunchy-gravel driveway. I smiled when I saw my cat sunning himself. He was a stray I found years before, while I was riding my horse on the back road to town. I heard a small meow coming from the brush on the side of the road. I saw a small tiger-striped kitten running after my sorrel mare. Naturally, it had to come home with me, so I turned the horse around and headed back to the house with the small stray safely cuddled inside my shirt. I announced to my surprised parents that "it had followed me home." They just laughed. I did too, later on. There was no way a kitten could have followed me home at that distance.

The most wonderful cat in the world; his name was Puud. He slept on my bed when he was old enough to jump that high. Puud had rules. One rule: No other cats - on my bed or in the house.

I am a cat person. In the years that followed, I married a Richard and found another cat, a grey Maltese named Clyde. I trained Clyde to walk on a leash. Tail held high, his fine hair would dance in the air when he moved. I took him on our trips and this time he went with me to Antlers where my parents lived.

It was evening and I was on my bed, with Clyde lying next to me, when I saw Puud sitting at the doorway to my room. His quiet slanted eyes silently stared at me. Clyde saw him first, jumped up, and ducked under the bed. Puud spread his sharp claws, took a flying leap and landed in my lap. I reached out a hand to pet him when, fangs bared and dripping with vengeance, he sank his teeth into the fleshy palm of my thumb.

Surprised, shocked, I lifted my hand thinking he would let go. He did not. I moved my hand trying to shake off the cat. No luck. I tried to pull his jaws apart with my left hand. No, I was locked in a vise. I called out to my husband and asked him to come help me.

When he didn't come, I raised my voice and said firmly and evenly, "The cat bit me. Come get him off!" Pain radiated in my hand because cat teeth clamped down on my bones. Richard entered the room, looked at the cat, then at me. I said, "Don't hurt him."

He grabbed hold of the cat's head and somehow pulled the cat's jaws apart. I looked at the cat before Richard let him go and he seemed all right. I knew enough to wash the wound. So off we went to the bathroom, where I sat on the lid of the toilet next to the sink, while Richard held my hand under the running water. By now my hand was throbbing, and the soap and water stung, I didn't faint or pass out. From the corner of my eye, I saw grey-striped Puud run to the back door and out of the house.

The next morning, the cat bite on my hand was sore but not infected. Richard, however, had been scratched and developed cat scratch fever. He was so sick that we needed to leave and get him to a doctor. He felt too bad to drive, so I drove the car home while Richard sat slumped in the passenger seat. He was in bed for a week and very miserable. I, on the other hand, felt fine. Today, when you look at my worn hand tanned by the sun, you will see a small white scar where a jealous cat bit me.

Diane Alexander Franke

The Rest of the Story

This supernatural experience happened while water was cleansing my cat wound, deep, moving, so personal, my heart is still silent. I now open my soul for you to see and experience what lies in the silence. I believe my spirit was taken back in time. . .

I seemed to walk on a rough dirt road. Warm air carried fragrances from flower-strewn hills, the sun not hot enough to sip the dew still cupped inside their petals. I wondered at the scent, it was too early for roses to bloom. Never mind, spring was ending gently, and the sky was scattered with clouds. A pleasant day holding promise of nights still crisp and cold. The road I walked on seemed familiar, dusty and rocky, well-traveled and early enough in the day that it was not crowded with travelers or Romans.

I moved behind a group of people and listened to their conversations. Feeling happy and with my friends. A few of our brethren had gone on ahead to find food and lodging for the night. Laughter broke out among some of the men who were engrossed in good natured arguing over something our Rabbi had said. These Talmidim, apostles, were dressed like most men of the Galilee. Plain garments worn with or without a girdle of leather or rope around the waist. The leather served to hold their clothes firmly when they gathered the hem of their garment and pulled it between their legs to tuck it in their waist (girded their loins), when they climbed, or entered water.

A few wore robes to keep them warm during the cold nights. The robe was folded and used as a pillow, or to soften the hard ground they often slept on. It was also spread across low branches to give them shade. Simple leather sandals protected their feet from sharp rocks and thorns. Several Hebrew men wore a tallit (prayer shawl) draped over their shoulder or arm. To protect their heads from the sun, they wore a cloth over their head, which was wrapped around their face and neck when dry winds from the desert blew fiercely. Simple men with simple needs. They wore a sharp knife that could be used for eating and a sheathed sword that was tucked in their girdle.

After walking a distance, we paused to rest, and drank deeply from a flask of water. When we had our fill, Yeshua (Jesus) began to speak to us in a soft, gentle voice about the God of Abraham,

Issac and Jacob. The tone of His voice invited us, he taught us how His Father wants us to live and think. He taught us common sense. Patient and firm, Jesus planted knowledge and the good news of the kingdom of heaven and made them safe in our heart. He filled us with wisdom. We were taught how to discern, what to speak and how to pray. We learned discipline, skills in listening, and how to see the truth.

Now, after emphasizing a point, He stopped talking to us. He turned his head with a solemn look in his eyes, tilted His head as if He were listening to someone we could not see, and talked in a voice so low we could not hear what was said. When He finished speaking, He looked at each of us and smiled.

Gratitude shone from our faces as we looked at Him. Soon though, He left us and walked a short distance, to be alone. We watched as He covered His head and face with His tallit, and quietly bowed His head in prayer and communion with His Father. As one, we covered our bowed heads and prayed.

Later, we listened as He talked about His Father's kingdom and spoke words that healed our personal wounds. Without a sound, He came to me. His warm eyes smiled into my heart and restored my soul. Cleansed, I wept behind my eyes. His rough, gentle hands moved in the air. He breathed on me, taught me, and sealed me. My time with Him was now over. My heart beating painfully, I hesitated, turned back and faced Him, held my hands out toward Him and silently asked if I could remain with Him and my friends. Glory, brighter than the sun, shone from Him. Son of God, all Heaven behind Him, spoke without sound, I must return.

I bowed my head and said to Him, "I will come here many times." Then angry because I could not stay with Him, I cried out in anguish and promise, "One day, I will come here and never leave."

But His Breath of Heaven seemed to move me forward in time, to return my spirit to my body. I reached out and turned off the faucet on the sink.

Light shines forever behind my eyes. The feeling when He looks directly into your eyes pierces your soul with Love. You are suspended in eternity and filled with Him. His Light and Power enters you. It is an intimacy that cannot be explained, only lived. It is sacred and holy. Truth.

I remember a warm day on two dusty roads. One dusty road where I found a soft kitten with sharp teeth and a strong bite that the Holy Spirit used to open a doorway to another dusty road where I walked with Jesus. In part, He has opened my soul to you. He gave me a gift of new life. His Word is written on my heart and body and sealed within me, to be released and shared with others.

Within me is a new heart filled with joy and gratitude for His gift, yet there is pain of separation from a time when He walked with me down a dusty road. He asked me to share with others what he has given me. He asks you to trust Him. Listen to Him, believe His words of life and repent.

Diane Alexander Franke

Beads to inspire:

Love

For God so loved the world that He gave His only begotten Son, that whoever believes in Him should not perish but have everlasting life.

(John 3:16 NKJV)

Wordwrights OKC Christian Writers presents:

Barbara Hernandez

After 40-plus years working in the insurance industry, Barbara Hernandez is looking forward to a retirement filled with lots of time writing for her family. With a passion for short stories and poems, the move from Vice President to Housewife/Writer holds the promise of being a very pleasant transition. Barbara has had a short piece published in We Will Never Forget, a collection of first-hand accounts of the 1995 Oklahoma City bombing. She has also had two poems chosen for online anthologies and was awarded two honorable mentions in the 2013 Art Affair poetry contest.

Home with Grandma Thomasson

"Don't eat the green-uns" she said as I sat in the middle of the large patch of cherry tomato plants. "They'll turn your stomach."

I turned my head toward the house to hide the bit of unripe tomato I knew must be showing between my teeth. All of the plump, juicy red ones had been plucked from the vines within my reach. I'd begun to settle for the ones with just a hint of pink to their skin.

Working in the garden with my grandmother was my favorite thing to do. No, that's not true. Learning new domino games like "42" or "Shoot The Moon" was my favorite. Grandma always let me shuffle the pieces with their smooth, glassy surface dimpled by the holes that had been counted time and time again. Actually, I think sitting on the floor at her feet while she read aloud from her vast supply of *Reader's Digest Condensed Books* was my number one favorite. Or perhaps, it was just being with Grandma that I loved so much.

Grandma's house was my refuge, my safe haven. Often, I escaped from my otherwise troubled childhood into the calm of that little home on 40th street. The house itself wasn't much to look at; a plain little white box with a porch and windows was all most would see. But to me, it was so much more. I never felt less than special when I was there.

Grandma took as much care with the tiny flower garden near the front steps as she did with the diverse mix of vegetables in the huge backyard. The patch of spindly, blue flowers she called Bachelor's Buttons had been split and shared with nearly every neighbor on the street. But then, so had baskets of zucchini squash, jars of green beans or pickles, and many other goodies that passed through Grandma's kitchen.

During the summer months when I often spent the night, Grandma would wake me early. Dressed in her standard uniform of apron and bonnet, she got her basket from the dining room and the little silver paring knife that was almost always lying on the rubber dish rack in the kitchen. With just a slight pause while she slipped her feet into the "mud-shoes" waiting next to the back door, we headed to the garden. The grass was wet and the sun hadn't been hanging in place long enough yet to warm our faces.

Picking cucumbers was my priority task. Grandma's back would ache far too long if she had to stay bent over the tangle of cucumber vines. I was supposed to pick them before they reached the length of my child size hand. Anything longer than my index finger should be gently pulled from the vine. Occasionally, I would find a giant cucumber hiding under the scratchy leaves. With my fingers barely able to go around its middle, I'd lift it up to show it off. Grandma said those were too big for pickles but just right for eating.

When the cucumber vines had given up all their bounty, I headed for the cherry tomato plants. These, Grandma planted just for me. She used the great big tomatoes for making chow-chow relish or for juicing or stewing, but the little round ones were for eating. They seldom made it into the house.

The stove that looked so big when I was a child, seemed to always have something boiling or roasting. Most mornings, she would count out four strips of bacon for the big, black skillet, and after pouring the grease off into a metal can in the middle of the stove, she would scramble four eggs in the drippings that still clung to the pan. Preparation of our garden goodies began as soon as the breakfast dishes were done. Whether we were freezing okra or canning green beans, she never lost her patience with my endless questions about what we were doing. Making pickles was my favorite. I still remember watching her turn the searing, hot glass jars upside down on the countertop. For the next few hours we would listen for the loud POP as the lids were sucked in by the vacuum created inside the jar. If one didn't pop, it went into the refrigerator to be eaten first.

When the summer months ended, I walked to and from school. It was just a short detour to Grandma's house where there was always a treat waiting for me. Some days it was a bowl of peach slices sitting in the freezer, needing only a splash of cream to complete the yummy, after school snack. The lone peach tree in the back yard was never strong enough for climbing but managed to provide enough furry little fruits to supply me and Grandma for several weeks during the summer months. Oddly enough, it wasn't the fresh fruit that I loved best. It still brings a smile to my lips when I think of the irregular-sized slices that Grandma packed into clear glass jars, covering them with a thick, sweet syrup.

When the weather turned cold, I anticipated the smell of homemade yeast rolls or the belly-warming magnificence of a bowl of rich, thick stew. On the days that chicken noodle soup was on the menu, I knew there would be a chicken neck with all the giblets sitting in a bowl. The little strings of meat needed to be pulled from the neck carefully, making sure none of the tiny bones got in the pile of tidbits that would be hand-fed to her dog, Trixie. Grandma could have taken care of this task earlier in the day as soon as the meat was cool enough to handle, but she knew I especially enjoyed this part.

Just before the sun's light faded completely, Grandma looked toward the door and said, "It's time." I recall the sluggishness of my movements as I gathered my things for the short walk home. Writing this, I ponder for the first time how much more difficult sending me home must have been for her than it was for me.

I don't remember many details about Grandma's house. I couldn't tell you how many windows were in each room, and I've no idea what color the walls were painted. The details I do remember are things that gave me comfort, things that even now cause my heart to swell until it pushes a little lump into my throat. Leaving the world behind when I stepped through her front door, I remember the home away from home that was built with Grandma Thomasson's love.

My Pickles

Cucumbers small,
Hang on the vine.
Soon will make pickles,
My favorite kind.
My Grammy picks
The ones that are tiny,
She packs them in jars,
With water so briny.
Mustard seed pellets
And dill that is fresh,
Only she could create
The ones I love best!

Barbara Hernandez

Ties That Bind

Thirty-two stories shake like Jello.
Source of the blast not yet known.
Then smoke appears giving way the location.
Precious minutes wasted, calling the daycare - on a useless phone.
Filled with fear.
Out of shape.
Running towards the commotion.
Not wanting to see what there was to find.
Unfamiliar emotion, my very being threatened.
I ran.
I panted.
I listened to the sound glass makes - when it grinds beneath your shoes.
"Where are the babies?" This mother's cry.
"There are no more babies." came the cruel answer.
Despair.
Desperation.
Decided denial.
An ambulance wails.
The sound goes unnoticed.
The babies are here! Round the corner, unseen.
There she is.
She lives.
The blood has clotted in her baby- fine hair.
New spring dress forever stained.
Shock.
Fear.
Disbelief.
Relief.
How similar they all seem now.
Her blood mingling with that of the transient that holds her.
His temporary room at the YMCA now part of history.
He smiles when he realizes I am her mother.
More meaningful words have never been spoken than in that silent expression.
The transition is made from his loving arms to mine.

Would I have cared so genuinely for this man yesterday?
A good Samaritan offers his cell phone.
Dazed, actually thinking it would work.
His starched white shirt is in shreds.
Blood covers his right side.
The collar, still crisp on the left, hangs limp with red on the right.
Why am I noticing this? What's wrong with me?
Help me, Lord.
The tree is on fire.
Cars exploding.
All unseen.
The contrast of this man's collar forever imprinted in my mind.
No tears.
Just the clinging of my baby.
Head nestled into the hollow of my neck.
Gentle cooing.
Attempts to soothe.
All at once, it occurs to me that I am making the noise.
Is it working?
Am I soothing her?
Am I soothing me?
The towel wrapped around her legs is soaked.
It sticks to my skin.
I pull it away from my arm and realize it is her dried blood that holds us together.
Ties that bind.

Barbara Hernandez

Beads to inspire:

Peace

These things I have spoken to you, that in Me you may have peace. In the world you will have tribulation; but be of good cheer, I have overcome the world.

(John 16:33 NKJV)

Wordwrights OKC Christian Writers
presents:

Joe Jared

Joe Jared writes historical novels, Christian devotionals, children's books, memoirs, and poetry. His most recent publication, Indigo Bunting, is a collection of 60 poems about different species of birds. His book, Polly's Little Universe, helps pre-teens develop critical thinking skills through a humorous, imaginative story. His memoir, Buzz, tells the story of his journey from atheism to Christ. Please visit Joe's website at joejaredproseandpoetry.com.

O Little Maid, Judean Maid

O little maid, Judean maid, what did
you think when you were told? Did angels come
to you before, when you were kneading bread
or when you ported water to your home?
Or were you working, brushing with your broom?
What flickered on the angel's face? A smile?
"The Holy Child will grow within your womb,"
He said, and you agreed though flesh is frail.
O Mary, did you fear that you might fail?
The wise brought frankincense and gold and myrrh.
His little hand will break from beneath a nail!
Your tender heart will break from grief and care.
O Mary, night is emptiness within;
He came to save His people from their sin.

Joe Jared

O Come and Honor Him

Gold is the gift for royalty, for kings.
It scatters amber sparks around the throne,
Reminding where the massive power clings.
O come and honor Him with precious stone.
But frankincense is for the priest alone,
diffusing prayer's aroma like a rose.
He prays, and gentle drops of blood atone.
O bring Him frankincense while mercy flows.
There's myrrh with agony that no one knows;
it winds the cloth around the corpse. It tolls
the bell. It writes redemption's rugged prose.
O take Him myrrh with trembling in your souls.
So come, wise men, from wandering and war
to give the Babe your gifts. Behold the star!

Joe Jared

Wordwrights OKC Christian Writers
presents:

Jody Karr

Jody Karr is an artist and photographer who writes fiction, non-fiction, and poetry. She has received national and international awards in art and national and regional awards in writing and poetry. She has served as judge for art, photography, and writing competitions. Jody has published numerous articles and a book of poetry entitled Faces Forgotten; her work is also featured in poetry books and anthologies. She is the editor for an international newsletter. Her art was included in *A Walk into Abstracts ... How Did They Do That* (2012, Sue St. John). Currently, Jody is working on three books and many art projects. Contact her at (405) 670-3142 or writer.artist.jody@gmail.com.

A Tribute to the Desert Queen

Oh trumpet queen of June
you one-night bloom in white
earth lies an eager canvas
on a fragrant summer night.

Your petals drink the moonlight
while the stars enjoy the view
through a window of melting time
framed in midnight blue.

I celebrate your beauty
a sight seldom seen
a mystery in the shadowy sand
oh sweet desert queen.

While the end draws near
your powers reach and flow.
On the sleeves of the wind
you slowly start to go.

Fragile lady in the night
how lonely you have been
grown by a hand unseen
you will return again.

Jody Karr

Midnight in the Garden

I bite into a raw tomato.
The rhythm of red tangos
on my tongue, dribbles.

Mango moonlight dances on the stars
white rhinestones in a ballroom sky.
Cucumber beckons greenly

waltzes through the air, ripe
breath upon my nose
midnight in the garden.

Jody Karr

Garden of Love

In the garden, petals tremble
spread eagerly, offering free
love, naked earth, flower power.
Grable stems, an Astaire flair stop
insects mid-air. Cotton candy
for their pleasure, edible rain.
Walls of Kermit green, burst of sun
shoulder to shoulder meet as one.

Jody Karr

The Way of Tides

Far beyond the sun-baked beach
past fishing shacks and lobster pots
lies a beaten bank of crevices
where the surf churns foam and breaks.

Low tides let me wander
into pocket worlds where the ocean plays.
I breathe salty mysteries as the
wings of the wind talk to the sea.

Starfish and anemones dine.
Seaweed hangs from rocks like
Rapunzel's locks, a pathway
of slippery velvet green.

Snails, whelks, barnacles and mussels
slurp, slither, cling, or glisten.
Glimpses of limpets and sea urchins
etch a quiet passage within.

The fading foam whispers – life is short.
Breathe it in faster, pounds my brain.
Like the waves, I know the way of tides.
High or low, their rhythm is mine.

Jody Karr

Autumn Ride

Winter's sleep beckons.
Leaves ride together,
speechless passengers
under whiskey skies.

One eye open, each
leaf stretches, breaks, leaps.
Landscapes come alive
while death feeds the earth.

Lemon-lime connect.
Cranberry-grape dance.
Leaves gather, scatter.
New life dines.

Jody Karr

Wordwrights OKC Christian Writers
presents:

Bonnie Lanthripe

Bonnie Lanthripe is a playwright, actress, and novelist with degrees in Theater and Creative Writing. She has written several one-act stage plays and Estate Sale, a full-length published work. Her short stories have appeared in inspirational, historical and devotional anthologies. Originally from Arkansas, she and her husband, Jim, made their home in California before moving to Edmond, Oklahoma. With four grown children and six grandchildren, Bonnie says there is always a story just around the corner.

Bonnie's Young Adult adventure/mystery novel, The Ringleader, was released recently, and she is currently working on its sequel.

Cactus by My Window

Three Christmas cacti reside year-round by my dining room window. They are well acclimated to the space and thrive there. One thing I learned when they took up residence is that all Christmas cactus are not created the same.

The largest of the three I inherited from my mother more than thirty years ago. Mom had a quirk for naming her plants and this particular one she called Henrietta. This grand old lady rarely bloomed when she came to my house, certainly not at the expected time – sometime in December, in time for Christmas. When January arrived, she might put on a few blooms, if she felt like it.

I propagated a second plant from a branch that voluntarily fell off Henrietta one day. The offspring became Henrietta II. Not very original, I'll admit. However, she sprouted easily and flourished quickly but was also slow to bloom, maybe some sparse blossoms sometime in February.

The smallest of the plants is Wanda. One summer, I visited a friend in California who had several pots of Christmas cactus in the courtyard by her front door. I snipped a sprig from one, brought it home to Oklahoma, and named it for my friend.

Wanda, the friend, has been an inspiration to me for many years. Facing life-threatening illnesses and tragedies with dignity, courage, and a radiant smile, she has been a model of faith and hope to all she comes in contact with.

There were three leaves on the small twig I put into soil in a small pot. I placed it near my kitchen window so I could keep an eye on it, praying it would survive. One day just before Thanksgiving, I walked into the kitchen to make morning coffee and received a delightful surprise. Wanda had only one spindly stem and three leaves, but each leaf bent toward the sun streaming through the window, each leaf tipped with a glorious pale pink blossom.

After praising her, I lifted the pot from the kitchen counter, took it into the dining room, and placed it on the window sill between Henrietta and Henrietta II. "There, ladies, *that* is how it's done," I announced and walked away. Wanda's blooms didn't begin to wither until after Christmas.

However, by that time there were brilliant fuchsia blossoms on mother and daughter. They even put on a second show around Valentine's Day. Wanda had done her job. The other girls only needed to be reminded – or inspired.

Wanda put on only a couple more branches over the past years, and is still quite small compared to the other plants. But every year since then, her white-tipped pink petals lead the way for the Henriettas to begin their show.

Each time I see the glorious matching display, I remember my dear friend. I can only hope to emulate her in my own life. To be an example to others with dignity and faith and hope.

I remember and I bloom.

Bonnie Lanthripe

Wheel of Life

When I returned to the classroom after a thirty year absence, pottery was one of the electives I chose to round out my required year-round, full-time schedule.

About that time, our youngest son changed schools and returned home to go to the same university I attended. I shared with him how much I was enjoying my classes and told him, "I think you would love pottery."

Being a Graphic Arts major, it was only a matter of time until he enrolled in a ceramics class. He was a natural. He became a true artist with a passion for his craft. By the time he left college, he had a following, was showing and selling his work, and presenting demonstrations.

The first time I attended one of those presentations, even though I knew most of the basics of the craft and had seen him work, I watched with fascination as he placed a melon-sized lump of clay on the potter's wheel. I listened with rapt attention as he described the elements that went into making the material pliable and useful. When he pressed the wheel into motion and it began to turn, he placed his hands on the clay, the strength of his hands firmly compelling it to yield to his control. Applying just the right amount of pressure, he centered the mass on the wheel.

"Sometimes," he explained, "the clay resists this part of the process, but unless it is properly and completely centered, it will be a struggle to complete a balanced useful piece. Almost impossible.

"The clay can take any of many different shapes," he went on as he worked. "A vase, a bowl or a cup, maybe a plate. It depends on what type of clay that is used and the method of firing. The choice is mine." While he talked, the mass beneath his hands began to expand as he masterfully pulled it slowly upward into a tall exquisitely-shaped urn.

When the wheel slowed, he used a tool to separate the large vase from the base before it stopped revolving. He removed it from the wheel and held an identifiable piece of pottery in his hands.

I 'oohed' and 'aahed' along with the rest of the audience before he said, "But this is not finished."

He went on to explain how the product he held was unusable in its present state. He would place it on a shelf in another room in a controlled environment. When it was thoroughly dry, it would be placed in a kiln and fired at an extremely high temperature, then glazed and allowed to dry again, and returned to the fire once more. The vase must be properly prepared, he explained, each step necessary, to ever become a serviceable product.

During the demonstration, my thoughts drifted back to when I had taken the pottery class. I found it therapeutic, but my efforts had produced small tight bowls and cups and dense heavy pots. At the time I struggled with the wheel. I struggled with the clay. And every day I struggled with physical, emotional, and spiritual pain.

Over the course, I came to realize my output was a reflection of my own inner condition. As I wrestled with the clay, the wheel, and all the personal issues confronting me, the Master Potter reminded me that I had once been like the clay, a clump of dirt made up of all the essential components yet without shape or purpose to my life. Resistant to His authority; defiantly challenging His purpose for my life; unwilling to yield to His plan.

Yet He never released His hold on me. Lovingly, He had firmly but gently led me to submit and yield my will to His and allow Him to center me under His control so I might be formed into the vessel He intended me to be.

I realized that just as I had chosen when I was young to trust Him to give my life genuine useful purpose, I knew I could trust Him to guide me through that trying time in my life. It was only the preparation process. He would be with me through the dry times, the dark times, the times of fire. It was His decision what kind of vessel I would become.

I can't say that my pots and cups and bowls ever resembled a work of art, but I have found uses for them around my house.

Next to my desk where I write, I have a very unusual, one-of-a-kind pencil holder as a constant reminder that my life is always in the hands of the Master Potter.

Bonnie Lanthripe

Wordwrights OKC Christian Writers
presents:

Donna Le

Donna Le's short stories are published in Oklahoma: The Fountain of the Heartland and Shades of Tulsa. Le's many years as a classroom teacher inspired her to write a middle grade novel, The Homeless Guy's Secret. Donna frequently speaks to various community groups, where "Lessons from the Heartland" is a popular presentation.

She can be reached at DKLE45@hotmail.com.

Christmas Treasure

For where your treasure is, there your heart will be also.
(Matthew 6:21 NIV)

Did you have a good Christmas? What did you get for Christmas? Was Santa good to you? We hear these questions every year. What is the right answer?

Could it be any of these? Toys, a skateboard, bicycles, a Barbie, a laptop, a Kindle, an iPad, a Smartphone, a digital camera, a gold chain, a diamond ring, or a car. What makes the best gift?

In our hearts, we know these gifts do not bring lasting happiness. Christmas is very important. We want to celebrate the birth of Christ. How do we avoid reducing the season to storing up treasures on earth?

Start with asking the correct question. Instead of "What did you get for Christmas?" contemplate "Do you *get* Christmas?"

Have you ever received a present wrapped so beautifully you didn't want to disturb the paper or bow? It's as if opening it would spoil the secret held inside. We can't imagine whatever is inside measuring up to expectations.

Jesus is the ultimate gift. Given to us out of love from our Heavenly Father, Jesus bestows the gift of love and eternal life. We have to open this gift daily to appreciate what we've been given.

God, Himself, came to save us. He walked on this earth showing us how to serve one another, how to have compassion for one another, and how to forgive one another.

He humbled himself and chose to be born, not in a palace, but in a stable. He was obedient to Joseph and Mary. The crown he wore was a crown of thorns. If we follow His footsteps and set aside earthly pleasures, we will be rewarded. In return Jesus promises joy, love, and peace. With Jesus we have a future, a home in paradise.

Do you *get* Christmas? Store up treasures in Heaven by being humble, generous, compassionate, charitable, kind, gentle, patient, and forgiving. Open your heart and you will receive the best present of all. What gift is better than being with Jesus for eternity?

Do not store up for yourselves treasures on earth, where moths and vermin destroy, and where thieves break in and steal. But store up for yourselves treasures in heaven, where moths and vermin do not destroy, and where thieves do not break in and steal. For where your treasure is, there your heart will be also.

(Matthew 6:19-21 NIV)

Prayer: *May I celebrate the true meaning of Christmas.*

Donna Le

Christmas Unclaimed

But the angel said to them, "Do not be afraid. I bring you good news that will cause great joy for all people. Today in the town of David, a Savior has been born to you; he is the Messiah, the Lord.
(Luke 2:10-11 NIV)

Year after year, the celebration of Christmas, for me, centered around fervent gift buying that started with after-Christmas sales and ended on Christmas Eve when the last store closed. I had an ever-growing list of family names, special friends, and co-workers that I spent time agonizing to find just the right present for each. When in doubt about my selection, I'd add extras – one of those mugs filled with sweets or a nice key chain or even a book.

As family members, we'd assemble at my mother's house, the growing pile of presents overpowering the tree. Quantity equaled love.

One Christmas Eve after the stack had been distributed and unwrapped, one lonely package remained on the decorated tree skirt. The designated "Santa" was unable to deliver the gift because it lacked a name tag. There it sat, solitary and unclaimed-until I uncovered a corner and sneaked a peek. The rightful owner then received her prize.

Several Christmas seasons passed before a decline in the economy caused our family to establish a new policy on gift giving. Adults would no longer exchange gifts; only the children would receive presents.

At first, I thought this new tradition would put a damper on the festivities. How would anyone know how much I loved them if I couldn't shower them with gifts?

To my surprise, I found myself focusing on the story of the nativity, and a joy entered my life that I had not expected. Gone was the mountain of gifts, replaced by time to visit family and friends. Time to shop for the Angel Tree. Time to transport shut-ins to view the lights they would not have otherwise been able to enjoy. Time to pour myself a hot cup of cocoa and reread the account of Mary and Joseph and the birth of Christ. Time to ponder the gift that our Heavenly Father gave us and time to invite the gift of Jesus into my heart.

When I think back on how I used to "celebrate" Christmas, I realize it brought no lasting joy, for nothing on this earth can fill the void if Jesus is not central in my life.

Distractions were removed. The focus is on Jesus. How would He want me to celebrate His coming into the world?

Jesus has transformed my life. The event of His birth brought me tidings of great joy. At my house, Christmas no longer sits unclaimed.

Prayer: *May I claim the gift of joy by accepting Christ in my life as my Lord and Savior.*

Donna Le

Wordwrights OKC Christian Writers
presents:

Andrea G. Moon

Andrea G. Moon is a Naturopathic Doctor. She is currently writing a book on natural health therapies in which she evaluates and reviews the latest alternative therapies in health and medicine. Her goal is to inspire readers to live naturally and spiritually!
She lives in Edmond, Oklahoma, with her four Yorkie companions and her husband. She can be reached at andehealth@yahoo.com or check out her website: www.drandreamoon.com.

My Dog Gave Me a Lesson in Faith

Missy, my Yorkshire terrier, was expecting her first litter of puppies. Our veterinarian had advised she have a caesarian due to the size of two of the pups. The procedure was scheduled for a Monday. The Thursday night before, three days early, Missy went into labor!

I had spent hours researching and planning for these puppies. When the vet said if she were *his dog* he'd go with the caesarian, I put aside all that planning work. Yorkshire terriers are supposed to have puppies in 63 days – Thursday was only the 60th day!

Now, I was suddenly thrown into recall mode! As I had researched, I realized the need for experienced help. Since Christians are to reach out to fellow believers for help, I had asked a friend, Rick, from my church community group to assist me. He lived close and was experienced with the birthing process of dogs. He had agreed and coached me on how important it would be for me to have a suction bulb syringe, used to clear nasal passages of newborn babies, and hemostats to crimp the cord.

An Internet search for puppy delivery turned up a whelping kit. Items in the kit included a birthing bed, towels, thermometer, scale, gloves, lubricating gel, and even a calcium supplement to boost pushing. I gathered all these things and cleared out a corner of my bedroom for the birthing area. Since it's very important to keep the puppies warm, I placed a heat lamp above the birthing bed and a thermometer to monitor the temperature.

I watched YouTube videos of Yorkie puppies being born, and even though I was fearful, I felt I was thoroughly prepared. I carefully calculated the due date. Rick agreed to be on call and ready to come over at a moment's notice.

On a cold February evening, I decided to check on Missy about 8:30 pm before watching TV with my husband, Larry. As I reached down to pet her, right before my eyes, her water broke! Her first contraction was like a wave on her body.

There was no time to call Rick. By the time Larry came into the room, the first puppy started to arrive. Half-way out, it stopped. After a few moments, I realized it was stuck. Missy was looking at me with so much ***trust*** in her eyes that I knew I could not fail her.

Without a whimper, she lay there trying to push the first puppy out. Outwardly, I was showing courage for Missy but inside, I was panicking. "Please God, give me calmness and courage to help Missy," I said to myself. If I showed confidence and courage to Missy, she would have confidence and courage too.

Remembering that the lubricating gel was for puppies getting stuck, I lubricated the puppy and all around the area, and then Larry pulled with gentle traction. All this happened so fast that Larry didn't even have time to put gloves on! It seemed like he pulled a long time before the puppy came out. The puppy didn't appear to be breathing fully, so we used the suction bulb syringe on him. I then called Rick, who was there within minutes and helped get the puppy breathing even better by turning him upside down and gently massaging him.

The next puppy also got stuck, but Rick knew what exactly what to do and gently helped pull the puppy out. Missy also knew exactly what to do. She cleaned the puppies and immediately started feeding them.

We named the first puppy Moses because he was the largest and the leader. The second puppy became Micah Angelo. We named the third Barnabas, Barney for short. The fourth puppy was a girl, very small and weaker than the others. We called her Sophia. The last puppy came just after midnight and we called him Benjamin, Benjie for short. Finally, Missy and her pups were out of danger and we enjoyed a moment of peace.

Reflecting on that night, I am reminded of 1st Corinthians 16:13-14: Be watchful, stand firm in the faith, act like men, be strong. Let all that you do be done in love (ESV). I was watchful over Missy and her puppies, acted with faith and strength from God, and all I did was in love.

The definition of faith is complete trust or confidence in someone or something. Missy showed me the meaning of true faith without complaining because she trusted me to help her. It's the same with God – we have faith in Him because we trust He will help us.

I learned a valuable lesson: Have faith and trust without complaining and call on friends (like believers) to help in times of need.

Faith draws us to trust God the Father, God the Son, and God the Holy Spirit. Know that we will have trials, disappointments and heartaches. Sophia, the tiny, weak puppy didn't survive. Still, with all our life experiences, we believe God is good and faithful. He will deliver us, take care of us – we are his children. We matter to Him, and our journey on Earth is temporary. We have eternal life if we place our faith in Jesus, trusting His death paid for our sins, and we will be forgiven and receive the promise of eternal life in heaven.

Acting with faith will lead you to joy, love and peace with God. My little dog delivered a big lesson in faith.

Andrea G. Moon

Beads to inspire:

Joy

Now may the God of hope fill you with all joy and peace in believing, that you may abound in hope by the power of the Holy Spirit.

(Romans 15:13 NKJV)

Wordwrights OKC Christian Writers presents:

Mona Jean Reed

Mona Jean Reed lives in Bethany, Oklahoma, and specializes in fiction and how-to-write fiction. Her novels, Reclaiming Little Marty and Snared, are in publication. A third novel with a working title of If It Kills Me is about ready.

In 2011, Mona Jean interviewed many WWII veterans and then published Freedom: A Salute to American Liberty. She writes a column on fiction writing and marketing. She also writes on inspiration, health, and gardening.

Mona Jean's main hobby has become learning "things." Her attitude is that if she doesn't know it, it's a good thing to learn. She was outraged to learn that slavery is still practiced in some parts of the world. For instance, it's legal in the Sudan. Here in America, there's a growing problem with sex trafficking, an especially hideous form of slavery. Innumerable people just disappear. Her novel, Snared, is a memorial to the abused and unknown lost ones.

In the Storm

May 31, 2013

"This storm is a killer!" The weatherman interrupted my TV show.

I flinched. That May in central Oklahoma, we had already lived through one F-5 tornado – at least, most of us lived through it. (An F-5 lifts houses off their foundations, makes matchsticks of them, and scatters them for miles.) We pay close attention to the weatherman because of these storms.

It had been a nice day. Then about three in the afternoon, the sky darkened. At six, the weatherman, with his colorful weather chart behind him, said, "This tornado is a monster." He pointed to a black area on his mostly-red map and said, "We're expecting golf-ball to baseball-sized hail. Anyone who isn't below ground if this comes their way, well, they just won't make it. Call your friends and relatives who are in its path. Warn them."

I've lived in the tornado-prone state of Oklahoma all my life and storms have never scared this seventy-six-year-old widow.

The weatherman estimated the storm would hit my town in thirty-two minutes. He said this tornado was a death sentence. I'm not sure whether I was angry at the storm or at the weatherman's pontificating voice, but I was angry. I was also determined to live—if the Lord let me.

The sky had already turned that peculiar shade of pale neon green that has indicated tornados since way before Dorothy and Toto rode a twister from Kansas to Oz. The weatherman repeated, "If you're not below ground, you won't make it." That did it. I have no storm shelter so I hopped in my car and boogied. After all, it wasn't like the tornado was on the next block. I had about twenty-five minutes to escape. Even an old woman can drive out of danger in twenty-five minutes.

The first drops of rain fell as I pulled out of my driveway. They predicted the tornado would follow a path about two miles south of my place—but being off-path by a couple of miles wouldn't be unusual. The tornado was south of me; I drove north, thinking I might never see my house again.

When I reached the first high traffic street that went north, I was so far back in line that I had to wait through three cycles of red and green lights before I could go farther.

While I waited, the first hail fell, but it only lasted a few minutes. When it stopped, I breathed a prayer of thanks. It had not broken any of my car's windows.

After the third red-green traffic light cycle, I reached the corner and decided that going east would be best since that street didn't have as much traffic and east was also away from danger. Two miles east, I turned north. The rain wasn't too bad; but hail pounded my roof. I had made my decision and had to live with the consequences.

Nothing looked normal in the weird neon green light and I lost my sense of direction. I drove down a wrong street and got lost in a neighborhood with twisting streets.

The hail beat on my car, but there wasn't a lot of it and it was only dime-sized. I thanked the Lord that I was still in one piece and so was my car.

Finally, I turned north on a major street and for a little while all was well except for the blinding rain. But soon, the water in the street rose until it covered the roadway from curb to curb, and I couldn't stop in heavy traffic.

I knew from past experience that wet brakes won't stop a car. As I had been taught years ago, I pumped and rode the brakes enough to squeeze some of the water out of the pads. Also, I avoided following close to the car in front of me because my stopping distance would be greater than normal until the brakes dried.

I refused to go into another twisty-streeted neighborhood. My only other choice was to keep going down that flooded street along with the rest of the traffic. At the same time, I prayed for the Lord to guide me. I sure didn't know what I was doing.

By now, the water was a bit more than mid-hubcap deep. I kept going for two more miles. Then I remembered that all the streets in that area went slightly uphill for another couple of blocks, and then they went sharply downhill. That street was about to become a car-swallowing lake. The tornado wasn't my problem anymore, but if I kept driving down this street, I'd still be in bad trouble. I needed an off-road shelter where I could wait out the storm.

It's miraculous, I made the decision to get off the road and immediately, there was a service station with an awning exactly where I needed it to be. There was one slot left, and I got it. At least I had no hail on three sides. It was the Lord's doing, not mine.

I spent an hour relaxing, praying, and listening to the radio's report of this awful storm. When the hail stopped, I decided to see if I still had a home.

Slowly, through mid-hubcap deep water, I made my way south. Finally, I reached the end of the flooded area.

At nine o'clock, I was only a couple of miles from my house. I drove down my usual access street until I came to a stalled car that was in top-of-tire, deep water. A one-eighty brought me to an alternate street.

The puddle that spanned most of that block didn't seem more than a couple of inches deep. After what I'd already driven through, I thought a couple of inches would be a breeze. Besides, I wanted to be home, if I still had one, so I plunged in.

I realized I could be in trouble when a couple of mallard ducks swam at my left elbow. The ducks kept swimming and I kept driving—fast to avoid stalling in deep water.

Thankfully, my house was in one piece. The next day, I saw no hail dings on my car.

I won't repeat this exodus maneuver the next time we have a tornado. You see, I made a mistake. Like everyone else, I occasionally forget that even public-spirited newspeople live by, "If it bleeds, it reads." Also, I should remember that weather excites weather-persons.

However it happened, I did more than survive. I found that with the Lord's help this old lady can still drive as well as most, better than some.

Now that it's over, I'll admit I was exhilarated. We all need to ride a roller coaster once in a while, even if it's just so we can remember how much we dislike riding them.

Praise the Lord for all His awesome gifts, even the storms of life.

Mona Jean Reed

A Cat Named "Cat"

We once had a cat named "Cat." We didn't intend to give him that name. But when this black-and-white kitten climbed my new drapes, "Cat!!" was what I shouted. He had a fascination with drapes and indulged it so often he decided "Cat!" was his name.

He was a good cat as cats go. Eventually he even learned not to climb drapes and to stay off the kitchen counter, even when no one watched him.

But, there were some things he never grasped. My hobby was painting. Cat knew he was not to go into my studio, but about every other week someone (usually me) left the door open. He would wander in and once in, he couldn't make himself leave.

Then he stood in the middle of the room yowling pitiably until someone shouted loud, frightening words that told him to leave. Poor Cat would scramble out as if his life depended on it. He'd hide under a bed for a little while, then he'd emerge, seemingly without remembering why he hid in the first place. If the door to my studio were open, he'd go back in and repeat the whole process.

In my opinion, ol' Cat had a rudimentary conscience. It worked just like any conscience. A conscience should to let us know when we're wrong. Humans are supposed to react by changing our behavior before our conduct gets us in trouble.

However, Cat's conscience only alerted him; he couldn't use it to free himself from that thing he knew he wasn't supposed to do. Animals need people to guide them for that reason.

Our conscience should work better than Cat's. When our conscience yowls, we can take the next step and remove ourselves from the dangerous place, person or attitude. We should feel a twinge of fear, leave, and vow not to repeat the experience. Unlike Cat, we don't need an external voice shouting at us—or worse.

So what's the moral of this little tale? Listen to your conscience. God gave us a conscience for our good. His Holy Spirit uses it to guide us. We follow His guidance and remove ourselves from bad things and head toward the good. It's the sane way to live.

But a conscience can only inform us if we listen.

When our conscience tells us of wrong thoughts or behavior and we refuse to stop, something terrible begins. If we persist in wrong actions or wrong opinions, our conscience weakens. It can die.

Cat was unusual. A normal cat has no conscience. If they wanted in my studio, it wouldn't matter how many times they'd been warned to stay out. They would sneak in, and probably scrub their cheek across a wet oil painting, ruining it. Then they would spoil other things by scrubbing that paint-marked cheek elsewhere. Too many people are like a normal cat. They can't tell what's right and what isn't. Their conscience is either dying or is already dead.

With a dying conscience, humans are blind and deaf to alarms, counsels and advice. But not knowing doesn't stop the calamities and unnecessary tragedies. If we survive, we call the disaster "bad luck." If we survive.

There is a cure for the weak and dying conscience.

The cure is Jesus. People who allow Jesus to be their Savior and Lord will find that soon their formerly useless conscience works as God intended. It warns of danger and helps with the process of heading to a better and safer place. An improved conscience is part of being a Christian.

God revives our dying consciences and gives real Christians the strength to overcome their wrong thinking and wrong actions. The Bible says: ***You are from God, little children, and have overcome them; because greater is He (Jesus) who is in you than he (the devil) who is in the world. 1 John 4:4*** (Above parentheses are for clarity only—not in the Bible.)

God makes us His children just as we are—warts, scabs, filth, and all. After we become Christians, we work at learning how to live close to God. That means we let Him be our Boss, every day and all the time. Through the conscience, God's Holy Spirit helps gossipers learn not to gossip and drug or alcohol dependent people learn to live haze-free. Lazy people, adulterers, liars, hot tempered people, fornicators and thieves find themselves similarly remade.

God never lets a Christian go. We might slip up and sin occasionally, but a real Christian's conscience won't let them habitually do things they know are wrong. 1 John 3:10 speaks to this issue: ***"By this the children of God and the children of the***

devil are obvious, anyone who does not practice righteousness is not of God, nor the one who does not love his brother."

Those who aren't Christian may feel they get away with their bad behavior. But God wants them to be His own dear children who are living the best life they can live for now and for eternity. Our black-and-white kitten lived to be nineteen. As obedient as a cat could be, he loved to curl up next to a human. Yet, nineteen years was all we humans could give him. God does far better for us; we get the whole of eternity to snuggle up next to God. And most wondrous of all, we're God's kids, not His pets.

In this sin-filled world, bad things are going to happen. When your ultimate bad thing – death – comes, your chance to become a Christian and live in heaven with Jesus will be gone forever.

If you decide you're not a Christian, and you want to become one, say a prayer something like this:

"Lord Jesus, I know that you died to pay for my sins. You are alive again because you never sinned. I turn from my sins and I make you my Lord, my Boss, my Savior and my Guide forever."

By saying words similar to these, and meaning them, you become a born-again Christian. The next step in your life as a Christian is to find a church that believes and teaches the Bible. Let the people there help you as you learn how to live a Christian life.

Mona Jean Reed

How to Lose Weight without Counting Anything

At thirty, I lost twenty pounds, from one-hundred-forty-five to one-hundred-twenty-five. I did it because my feet hurt. I had pretty well kept the weight off until about ten years ago. I was sixty-five at that time. My husband was ill and I watched TV with him a lot. That's when I slowed down on my exercise. Because he needed to gain weight, and because I was a good wife, by the Bible's definition (not the television one), I larded our entertainment with chips, dips, cookies, cake, and ice cream. The result was that I gained ten pounds over the same number of years.

I had a problem. You see, both the Lord of life and life itself have taught me that my frame is built for a max of about one hundred-twenty-five and a little less is good. Unfortunately, losing those ten pounds by dieting failed due to my poor discipline.

At one hundred-thirty-five pounds, my feet didn't hurt as they had when I was thirty and lost that twenty pounds, but they were beginning to groan. Besides, either I lost ten pounds or I had to give up my size ten to twelve wardrobe. I was now a widow and with social security as the biggest portion of my funds, my budget was as tight as my waistband. I couldn't afford to buy a complete set of new clothes.

Finally at the age of seventy-six, I lost that weight. To do it, I counted nothing, not calories, fat grams, protein grams, carbs, diabetic points, WW points, or anything else. I didn't even measure portion size in inches. If you want to try my "no counting" method for losing weight, here's what you'll need:

(1) A steno pad or other notebook which will be used only for this project and an ink pen. Keep the pad and pen next to your scale.

(2) A scale that has a digital readout that includes both the whole number and a tenth beyond. The weight on the digital readout will look like this: 125.8. I think these more accurate scales are necessary for the project to work. It's too easy to make excuses (lie to yourself) when using a less accurate scale.

I bought my second digital scale in the middle of 2013 for $25.00. There were some a little cheaper and many that were more expensive. My first such scale cost about the same and I bought it a year earlier. However, that first scale had a serious flaw. It used a watch battery that was secreted deep inside the "works." I broke the scale while trying to replace that tiny battery. I had already had some weight-loss success, so I bought a second scale right away. This one uses ordinary AAA batteries and they replace easily. I suggest you make sure your scale's batteries are easily replaced. You'll use your scale so often that you'll need to replace the batteries once in a while.

Now you know about the tools. Here's how you use them.

First: Every morning without fail, after your wake-up trip to the toilet and before you drink anything, weigh yourself on your digital scale. I suggest that when you step on the scale, you wear as little as possible. I take off my watch and house shoes and only wear my nightgown. Whatever you decide to wear while on the scale, it should be approximately the same weight each time. Since you could be doing this for years, simplicity has advantages.

Then I immediately record my weight. Consistency is important. If I had false teeth, I would have to decide whether to weigh with or without them and always weigh one way or the other. The same goes for curlers, hairpins, glasses or anything else.

Second: Every evening without fail, after all preparations for bedtime have been made, including that last trip to the toilet, step on the scale. Again, I wear only my nightgown, no watch, no house shoes, or anything else that could be eliminated. Then I immediately record my weight. Uniformity is essential.

In my weigh-ins, I see a consistent pattern of about two pounds greater weight in the evening than in the morning. (Example: A.M. weight: 125.6; P.M. weight 127.2. Next day: A.M. weight 125.4; P.M. weight 127.0.) When you state your weight to anyone, of course you give your A.M. weight.

That's all you do. Just record your weight with extreme accuracy morning and night. I fail to do even that much once or twice a month.

I think I know why this method works. As I developed this weigh-in habit, I found myself thinking things like: Do I really want that second helping? Or that cookie? Or, why don't I have broccoli with a very small amount of cheese sauce instead of mashed potatoes and gravy? When I cook I ask, is there a way to get this taste with less fat or sugar?

These more accurate scales are excellent tools. They provide feedback and encouragement that no diet plan gives me. I plan to weigh-in indefinitely to maintain my new weight.

I haven't covered a few things that would be helpful for you to know.

First, there are some physical issues that will cause my weight not to follow the two pounds greater in the evening pattern. If you notice, say, only a pound or less difference between the A.M. and P.M. weights and you <u>know</u> you haven't overeaten, just be patient and continue your A.M. and P.M. weigh-ins. The two-pound difference, or whatever is normal for you, will reassert itself.

Also, be sure to get rid of your "too big" clothes immediately. As an intellectual hobby, I've talked diet information with other women all my adult life, and I've never known anyone to keep their new weight if they kept their old clothes. Even if your new clothes come from a thrift store, keep only a wardrobe that fits your new, more slender, form.

One last thing, what if you're overeating regularly?

Well, it's your body…

However, diabetes, joint pain, heart attacks, and all the other sicknesses in which overeating plays a role are obviously destructive. So, when you have an urge for that extra brownie and you don't think you can resist, yet you know it's bad for you—guess where that urge is coming from? Hint: It's not from God.

God's nature is to heal and to grow things. Only when those who are His have been damaged and He must fix them will He cause pain—but even then, it's the pain of setting the broken part, perhaps the irritation of a cast or the growling of an empty stomach. For His people, only good things come from Him. If you need fixing, God's method may not be pleasant at the moment, but He never steers toward destruction anyone who is His.

I think the solution is to ask God for grace and strength to overcome the destroyer while you work on your weighty issue.

Mona Jean Reed

Luke 11:5-8 (Updated)

Tap, tap, tap.

I swam out of a sound sleep and stumbled toward my front door. On the couch in the living room, my two-and-a-half-year-old granddaughter, Amanda, slept.

As I passed by, I checked the table that I'd moved in front of the couch to keep her from falling. I was thankful that she stayed asleep in spite of the knocking; Amanda was an energetic handful.

I said I'd keep her while my son, Gary and his wife, Emma, took a romantic, week-long cruise. When I said it, I didn't think about the strain on me and my one-bedroom apartment. Of course, even if I had thought about it, I'd have said yes. The day they got married, I told God that if it killed me, I would be there for them. They needed this holiday.

Besides, this week only had three more days in it. I'm a strong old gal and I loved my little dynamo of a granddaughter. She wouldn't kill me; it only felt like it.

Tap, tap, tap.

Quick, before the tapping woke Amanda, I stopped musing and hurried to see who would come to my door in the middle of the night. First, I used that convenient peep-hole to make sure it was safe to open the door. Jody Carpenter, my good friend and next door neighbor, stood there. I thought she might have been hurt or her apartment was about to explode, who knew with Jody. Scatterbrain Jody didn't seem to have been in an accident.

I opened the door a crack and hissed, "Go away, Jody."

Amanda whimpered in her sleep. I really didn't want to rock her to sleep twice in one night, but if Jody didn't go away I'd have to.

Jody pleaded, "My friend, Brenda, just came in from Chicago and I wasn't expecting her. My cupboard is bare. You got something I can feed her?"

"Go away!" The nerve of the woman. I wanted to slam the door, but closed it softly. Mustn't wake Amanda.

Jody knocked again.

"Go to 7-11; get some donuts. Don't knock again." I forgot about Amanda and slammed the door.

"Mommy!" Amanda cried.

I hustled to the couch. Maybe I could get her back to sleep before she really woke up.

This time, Jody punched the doorbell and Amanda screamed.

I ignored Jody and picked my grandbaby up. "There, there, honey."

Amanda screamed and screamed again. That's when I realized she wasn't fully awake.

"It's all right, babe. It's all right. You're having a nightmare. That's all."

The doorbell rang again and the child not only screamed, but she hit at me, landing a good blow on my glasses. That hurt my nose so bad, I almost dropped her.

I gritted my teeth and carried Amanda while rocking her in my arms. Despite my little burden, I threw the door wide open.

Jody had her finger on the doorbell, ready to ring it again.

"Don't you dare punch that button!" I whispered. "Come in."

Just then, Amanda really woke up and became her usual energetic self.

"Down, Gramma. Want down."

I put my squirming grandbaby down and frowned at my so-called friend. "Now, you've done it. She won't sleep another minute tonight, and she'll be cranky from ten o'clock in the morning until bedtime."

"But, about Brenda. I don't want to send her away hungry."

Jody would be so hurt if I refused her.

Amanda ran ahead of us into the kitchen, opened a cabinet, pulled out two pan lids and marched around the apartment while banging them like a pair of cymbals.

Over the one-child-band, I shouted, "I've got to stop her before grouchy George sues me for excessive noise."

"But, Brenda's hungry and…"

"I've got half a cake and a little ice cream. They're in the fridge. Help yourself."

"Uh, thanks. You're a really good friend. I'm in your debt," Jody said.

"You've used just about every cent in your my friend account." She didn't hear me and that was just as well. I felt as cranky as Amanda would be in the morning.

I grabbed a coloring book. "Here you go, babe. Let's color!"

When Amanda stopped banging, I removed one of the lids from her sweet, but oh-so-stubborn hand and shoved a fistful of crayons in its place.

From the fridge, Jody said, "Almost forgot. I'm out of eggs. Don't suppose I could borrow a couple of eggs and maybe some of that sausage?"

I sighed, "Go ahead. Get them while you're in there."

"Some bread, too?"

"Take my last can of biscuits. Amanda likes to eat breakfast at McDonald's." I shouldn't have mentioned that fast food place.

My grandbaby perked up, "Micky D?" Then she jumped as if she had springs built into her feet. "We go Micky D!" She threw her crayons into the air and ran to get her shoes.

I repeated my vow to God, "Lord, I *will* encourage Gary and Emma. My beautiful little tornado *won't* kill me. I *am* a strong old lady. You made me that way."

I thought about what I'd just said for a few seconds and added, "Thank You, for all your blessings, Almighty God!"

Mona Jean Reed

Losing a Temper

I've wrestled with my temper for almost as many years as I've been alive. When I tell people that, most people don't believe me. That's because having a visible temper in my childhood home caused me so much pain that I learned to keep it under wraps. I'll bet I could out poker-face any millionaire who earned his money at the table.

I say the above as a word of caution. Just because others don't explode into an epic rant or grab the nearest table leg as a weapon doesn't mean they aren't angry.

What I learned in my childhood home is today called "stuff it."

A person who follows the "stuff it" advice has several problems:

(1) Anger doesn't go away. It festers at the root of a person's consciousness, like pus in a boil, waiting for enough pressure to explode.

(2) "Stuff it" gives the angry person a bottomless feeling of hurt. This is because their pain has no value. If people identify with their pain and it has no merit, they believe they have no significance. The lack of worth throws salt on the anger wound.

(3) "Stuff it" people desperately want repayment for their pain. Unfortunately, no one ever has enough of anything to repay the person who "stuffs" their anger.

Some possible results are cynicism, stress, fear and even bullying, usually in a sneaky, adult form that's difficult to guard against. Worst of all, people who "stuff it" tend to have a closed mind that allows little or no creativity. This lack of creativity and spontaneity causes them to seem less intelligent than they really are.

The more common advice about anger one might hear today is, "Let it out; don't stuff' it." This is bad advice. A person who follows the "let it out" advice will have their tantrum and perhaps they will get vindication from their outburst – but probably not.

Here is what happened on the few occasions when I've followed this advice:

(1) I looked like an out-of-control fool.

(2) I stiffened the resistance to giving me what I wanted or needed.

(3) In the heat of my temper, I used hurtful words and made enemies when people had either been friends or neutral toward me.

(4) I had to apologize, a painful process that didn't help my psyche.

(5) I felt less confident than before my tantrum.

(6) "Letting it out" one time made it much easier to "let it out" again.

One more point on "letting it out." I've watched a few people who let it out regularly. Am I saying enough if I quote from Proverbs? "Don't rescue an angry man; you will only have to do it again."

There is a third kind of advice that psychiatrists and psychologists are giving their clients. The Bible gives the same advice.

For instance, Abraham and Lot had too many sheep and cattle for one area. Abraham, as the patriarch, could have pulled rank on his nephew Lot and taken the fertile valley around Sodom for himself. He didn't; he let his self-centered nephew have that more fertile land and he took the leftovers.

And, Moses, the only man except Jesus with whom God ever talked face to face, was the meekest of all men. Moses' only known temper tantrum caused him not to follow God's instructions. He was not allowed entry into the Promised Land because of it.

In the Lord's Prayer, Jesus said, "Forgive us our trespasses as we forgive those who trespass against us." The word used for forgive means to release, to loose, or to let go. A Christian is to behave as a little Christ. We know how Christ reacted. In the midst of His torture on the cross. He said, "Father, forgive them, for they don't know what they're doing."

With those words, Christ released the hate-filled religious men who engineered His death and the spineless politician who allowed it. Christ didn't hold His flogging against His expert pain-givers. (Many of those sentenced to crucifixion died of the pre-crucifixion flogging.) Jesus didn't call down fire on the men who nailed Him to that wooden beam or on those who gambled for His clothes.

When the Father turned away because He couldn't bear to see His Son become the sin-bearer, Jesus didn't blame or fault Him.

We Christians have His clear example. We need to release those who hurt us. Our reward, whether given here on earth or in heaven or both will be great.

By the time a person is my age (old), several people will have done things that in one sense or another are close to unforgivable. It can't be helped. It's just part of fallen human nature; people hurt people on purpose or by accident.

We have choices. We can treasure up those hurts and insist on repayment. If so, we lock ourselves away from God's bright love and live in our tiny, dank place of pain and revenge. Or we, the hurt ones, can let the offending person go free and not even owe us a smile. In that case, we walk out into the light that God so graciously supplies.

How do you forgive? Ideally, the other person and I would meet face to face. I would tell them how they hurt me and say, "I forgive you." To date, this has never happened to me and probably won't. Why? People react badly to being accused. The other party most likely would become angry, thereby creating a worse situation. Of course, if an ongoing problem needs to be dealt with, confrontation would be necessary, even if the other person did become irate.

For every other insult or injury, I go with 1 Corinthians 6:7. There, Paul tells the believers to let themselves be cheated, if necessary, to avoid a problem in the church.

Another reason for not saying, "I forgive you," in person is that most of those who hurt me did it when I was a child and couldn't defend myself against adults. They are now deceased.

So, if a hurt that was done to me in the past comes into my consciousness, I say to God, "Father, forgive them." I still have occasional episodes of what amounts to a mild form of PTSD, but it's okay. I know it comes from my past, and I do my best to keep my past in the past. *Forgetting the past*, I press on toward the mark of the high calling of Christ Jesus. (Philippians 3:15)

Whether the hurt happened ten minutes ago or in childhood, the key is to say and *mean,* "Father, forgive them." As a reward after forgiving someone, I recommend doing something enjoyable, positive and non-fattening. *Mona Jean Reed*

Beads to inspire:

Love

Now hope does not disappoint, because the love of God has been poured out in our hearts by the Holy Spirit who was given to us.

(Romans 5:5 NKJV)

Wordwrights OKC Christian Writers
presents:

Rosalyn Reiff

Rosalyn Reiff has written in journals for over 40 years and has been published in several magazines and textbooks. As a short-term missionary, she taught English as a Second Language in Japan for three years, and later taught ESL at three colleges, elementary, middle, and high schools.

In Japan, Roz began to write haiku and enjoys writing other kinds of poems. She has done freelance editing for CourseCrafters, Inc. and hopes to write a humorous children's book.

Roz and her husband, Jon, live in Edmond, Oklahoma, and have three daughters, five granddaughters, one grandson, and one great-granddaughter. In their free time, Roz and Jon enjoy going to operas, taking walks at Lake Arcadia, and traveling to Europe and the Caribbean.

Treasured Ocean Days

I love summertime at the sea!
Roaring, rolling turquoise waves,
Soaring seagulls cawing through the skies,
Soft sand underfoot and between the toes,
Four giggly girls, dashing through the crashing waves.
Racing to catch up, one just-turned-three, curly-blond boy.
Laughing, splashing, tossing a beach ball,
Making sand castles, searching for sea shells,
Delightful days at the sunny seashore make us happy!
Each morning, eager to greet the dawn,
Sneaking past sleeping kids on the sofa bed,
With a mug of hot tea, and a Bible under my arm,
I slide open the balcony door
And marvel at the pink and purple swirls in the sky.
As the waves rise, fall, and thunder ashore,
I delight in God's exquisite creation,
And thank Him for forever memories.

Rosalyn Reiff

If Only

He putters around the yard,
Snapping off dried-up flower heads,
Yanking out gangly, wilted weeds,
Wandering about the lush green, fresh-mown grass.
Aimlessly roaming, leisurely inspecting,
Anything to keep him out of the house.
For thirty-five years, he loved her dearly.
So sweet and gentle, a woman of faith,
Cheerful grandmother, generous friend,
But a second round of cancer took her.
The house is . . . deafeningly. . . quiet . . . now,
Not even a tick-tock
Tapping from the grandfather clock,
No laughter bouncing off the walls,
No arias echoing through the rooms.
She and the happy life they shared. . . gone!
If only she would pop around the corner and say once more,
"Time for dinner, Honey."
If only he could put his arms around her one more time,
And say, "I love you, Sweetheart."
The silence loudly gongs as he softly pads
From one empty room to another.
If . . . only. . . she. . . were. . . still. . . here!

Rosalyn Reiff

For Love of Family

On a rainy November afternoon in 2008 in South Korea, Gukhee Hwang was driving her daughters to a doctor's appointment. While stopped at an intersection, they were hit when a huge truck suddenly rammed into the back of their car. After the jolt, her young daughters cried out but seemed to be okay. Gukhee managed to call her husband before she blacked out.

When she came to, she found herself in a hospital bed in serious condition. Her husband told her a drunk driver had dozed off and rear-ended her. She had a terrible headache from a concussion, her shoulders were injured, her back hurt, and she couldn't stand up, let alone walk.

For weeks, Gukhee couldn't remember things she had seen or recall information she had read. She repeated meaningless words over and over. Because of the terrible pain, she had to take strong pain killers by injection--five different ones every day to get relief.

She endured weeks of physical therapy through the severe pain. Thinking of her family, she worked hard, doing her best to regain her health and strength. However, in spite of all her efforts, she could do little for herself. She couldn't even pick up a pen or a spoon and had to take medicine to make it through the unbearable pain and then lie in bed after each treatment. This was her new hospital life, and she soon became very depressed.

She felt guilty and useless because she couldn't take care of herself and her family. She loved them very much, but they couldn't live as a family because of her disability. Her daughters were sent off to her mother's home, but they often called and said, "Mommy, we want to be with you. When can you come get us?" Her husband faithfully came to the hospital to see her every morning before work and every night after work.

Because they had to live in separate places, Gukhee, her husband and daughters missed each other very much. As the weeks turned into months, Gukhee felt as if she had forever lost her precious family, and did not want them to have a tough time anymore because of her. She felt her body getting addicted to the pain medicines. After four months of suffering, she lost all hope and wanted to escape from it all. She loved her family, but she couldn't stand the pain and detested her uselessness.

Before the accident, Gukhee disliked Christians, but her husband's sisters used to wake her up every Sunday morning and made her go to church. She had worked hard for the Samsung Company all week, and just wanted to sleep in on Sunday mornings. After the accident, she became furious with God! She had worked hard taking care of her children and parents. Once capable and hard-working, now she was totally helpless. The accident took away her family, her life, and her happiness. Being in this desperate situation, Gukhee knew she had one decision to make: either live or die!

Each day, Gukhee felt more hopeless and more depressed. Every day she cried and cried. One day, she decided to reject every pill and not eat anything. She got thinner and weaker; she planned to die and end it all.

One night soon afterwards, God, dressed all in white, came to Gukhee in a dream. "He looked at me and put His hand on my head and said, 'I see you all the time, Gukhee, and I know what a difficult time you are having. Don't be sad any longer. Don't be worried about your condition any more. You are going to be okay.'" Gukee will never forget when He came and spoke to her. It was impossible for her to describe how she felt.

When Gukhee woke up the next morning, she threw away all her medicines. Her doctor told her she had been made crazy because of the pain. He said she had seen an illusion, and would have to take stronger medicine than before. If not, she might never walk again, and her brain function would always be impaired.

But Gukhee focused on what she had seen and heard in her dream. She focused on God's words to her and determined to get better for her family. Because of her heavenly visitor's words, she began to focus on positive thinking rather than on pain and weaknesses. One night, she remembered a childhood dream—she wanted to be an English teacher. That night, a voice shouted at her, "You're crazy! You're disabled! You can't do that!" She told the voice, "No, I'm going to be okay. God told me that. I can be an English teacher! I will realize my dream."

Each day, rather than depending on medicine, Gukhee worked harder with the physical therapist to get her body to move. At first, she tried walking on her own – it took an hour just to take ten painful steps. When she tried to move her legs and walk, she fought for breath because of the pain, but because of God's promise, she did not give up!

Gukhee worked hard trying to remember what she read and what she saw. Because of her daughters, she read a book every day, even though she forgot most of it. A year later, she could remember almost 50% and two years later, almost 80%. It was all hard work, but she kept at it. She couldn't forget what God had told her, and she was determined to recover for her family!

Gukhee's doctor told her she could be disabled the rest of her life because of the accident. But in May 2014, six years after that traumatic time, she spoke at a Friendship International meeting in Edmond, Oklahoma:

"Look at me! I can walk! I can speak! I can remember what I did and what I read! My doctor and the finest medicine could not cure me! No, God healed me just as He said He would!"

Not only did God heal Gukhee, but He gave her new hope and new peace.

Gukhee began studying at the University of Central Oklahoma in Edmond, Oklahoma to be an English teacher! Though sometimes parts of her body still ache, she isn't worried any more. She's no longer afraid to live because she believes in God and knows He is always with her. As long as she trusts Him absolutely and doesn't give up hope, He will always take care of her and her family. Although Gukhee endured a lot of suffering, she and her family are happy about this miracle of God! They know now a joy they would never have known if she had not been plunged into hopeless despair.

Rosalyn Reiff

Voice in the Night

"You don't need that," said the doctor,"
nodding at my cane. "I'm right here."
It was like the voice I heard in the night,
"You will walk again!"
In late March, the strong Oklahoma wind
blew me over sideways.
Nothing broken, but leg bruises
and a fear of falling again.
Feet planted firmly on the floor two-feet apart,
I waddled forward.
Fear of more injury. "I need my cane!"
But the voice in the night said,
"You will walk again!"
"Oh, but I can't."
"Oh yes, you can!" He answered.
"Get up and walk," Jesus once said.
Do I dare trust Him?
And then the taunts from the enemy,
"You'll never walk again…Look at you."
"Where's my cane?" I wondered.
"You won't have the courage
to get up and walk," he continued.
"Do you know who you're talking to?"
I said. "I'm a child of the living God!
And did you know that with God,
nothing will be impossible?
I choose to believe His voice in the night."
"Oh yes, I'll walk again," I said.
"And I'm gonna drive, too.
You just wait and see!"

Rosalyn Reiff

Wordwrights OKC Christian Writers
presents:

Barbara Shepherd

Barbara Shepherd is an award-winning artist and writer of fiction, non-fiction, and poetry. She is the recipient of nearly 300 writing awards in fiction, non-fiction, screenwriting, and poetry, has won the American Christian Writers "Writer of the Year" (twice), is a "Lone Stars Poet," a "Woody Guthrie Poet," and a former nominee for Poet Laureate of the State of Oklahoma.

Shepherd has been a field editor for *Taste of Home* magazine. Her work is featured in books, literary journals, and magazines. Books in print include: Voices in Time, A Centennial Celebration of Oklahoma Stories, State Cops Cooking in the Heartland, Imagination Turned Loose, Beads on a String = Peace, Joy, and Love, and Patchwork Skin.

She founded and sponsors Art Affair Annual Literary Contests (www.shadetreecreations.com) for poets and writers – now in its tenth year. Her new website (www.barbarashepherd.com) is, like her life, under construction.

Taffy Pull

Marcy looks like a model, natural blonde curls cascade down past her waist. She's pleasant, smart, vivacious, has a positive attitude and her own signature style of dress. But she has a serious side – when it comes to Christianity.

Insincere people who wear their religion on their sleeves, spouting verses and beliefs at every turn, but displaying non-Christian and sometimes immoral actions can undermine a person's faith. But, Marcy is different; she means what she says and lives a true Christian life. Wary the first time we met, I was a little concerned about her until I spent more time around her and saw that her actions matched her beliefs. We became friends and I invited her one year out to the farm where I grew up.

The smell of boiling candy permeated the back room of Grandpa's house. Coming from the hot kitchen in the ancient split-log portion of the farm house, the odor transformed the cold back room into a party atmosphere. Grandpa brought his old hay hook in from the barn, scrubbed it clean and shiny, then dried it with a striped dishtowel.

He reached high to hang the iron tool on a huge nail, attached to a clean and heavily-varnished wooden plank on the sturdy wall. When Grandma brought in steaming, molten candy on a large cookie sheet, Grandpa buttered his strong, weathered hands and gathered up the hot taffy, too blistering for anyone else to handle. Exhibiting his years of experience, he slapped the taffy onto the hay hook and pulled it like a rope, repeatedly looping the heavy mass over and pulling it from the iron tool with a rhythm that bordered on grace. After the taffy cooled somewhat and Grandpa tired, he asked Marcy if she'd like to pull.

"I'd love to," she said.

He stepped away and she buttered her hands. But, before she could start pulling the heavy rope of taffy, Marcy, of course, had to pray over it!

Grandpa's terror showed in his chiseled face, and his eyes looked like they could shoot daggers. We all knew that you couldn't let the taffy cool without working it or it would harden into a giant glob. Not only would that ruin the candy, but his prized hay hook would be out of commission until we could chip away the rock-like candy with a hammer and chisel.

While Grandpa glared at his strange guest, the rest of us held our breaths, afraid our festive atmosphere had slipped into fuel for a fight.

Un-phased, Marcy concluded her prayer, verbal of course – she never did anything in silence. She stood on a wooden stool, stretched her butter-lathered hands to the still-hot candy, and belted out a couple of hymns while she pulled taffy until it was ready to slide off the hook for the last time.

Grandma came forth then to receive the "blessed candy," stretched it into a long rope, curled it back onto the cookie sheet and cut it into bite-sized pieces. We all enjoyed our taffy that year and remember it now, not as holiday candy, but as "Holy Taffy."

Barbara Shepherd

Author's Note:
For a great writing prompt, choose two characters who could never meet, and center your story or poem around them. I met Marcy long after my grandfather passed away, but "Taffy Pull" is probably what would have happened if they had faced one another at my family's Christmas event.

Unaware

… and a little child shall lead them. (Isaiah 11:6 KJV)

Attending Sunday School and church every week, for some, is as natural as a Sunday dinner of fried chicken or pot roast. For me, going to town to attend services was an ordeal. Although our neighbors offered rides to church for my brothers and myself, our attendance was sporadic, because permission to go was limited.

However, my mother took us to Bible School every summer and stayed at the church where she helped in the kitchen. When we made crafts, she joined us. Many summers, we learned a craft we wanted to continue at home – like leather tooling. Mom and I made a lot of wallets, key cases, purses, and belts for gifts. Sometimes, we would all go to Sunday School, but we seldom stayed for church service.

One Sunday, I had ridden to church with neighbors, and God spoke to my heart. I tried but could not ignore the pastor's invitation that compelled me to walk down the aisle to be saved. While tears of joy streamed down my cheeks, the pastor told the congregation I would be baptized in two weeks.

When I cry, red splotches cover my face and take hours to fade, so when I returned home, my mother demanded answers. She yelled at me. "What did they do to you?"

"They didn't do anything, Mom. I've been saved." I tried to explain it, but the experience proved difficult to put into words.

The following Sunday morning, Mom, my brothers, and I attended Sunday School and stayed for church. When we sang the hymn of invitation, my mother and all three of my tall brothers walked down the aisle to accept salvation. The five of us were baptized that next Sunday evening.

Prayer: *"Lord, guide us in our decisions, because we have no idea how much influence You might place in our actions. Amen."*

Barbara Shepherd

Butterfly Garden

Although it's autumn,
I watch a parade of butterflies
fly in and fold their wings
to drink nectar from new blooms of red, yellow
and magenta zinnias. Then, the winged beauties congregate
on huge coneflowers of faded cream and lavender.
The flower bed is a tangle of survivors from past weedings,
the last blooming stalks now drooping and turning brown.

I didn't plan a butterfly garden this year – just flowers
to complement my hibiscus and a few rosebushes.
What came were colors so vibrant everyone noticed them
while whizzing by on the street – you could hear
their engines slow for a better view.
Enjoying the riot of color most were those religious
with their morning jog and those who strolled by
every evening on my curved sidewalk.
Planting only from seed, I watched all varieties
reach for the sky. Coneflowers advertised
to reach three feet attained six and seven.
I'm glad I didn't fertilize because
what should have been eighteen-inch zinnias tripled in size.
Dwarf marigolds exploded into borders of yellow, orange
and burgundy – two feet taller than predicted.

I'll go out soon, with clippers, to snip dry heads
and save paper-thin petals of seed, though I
may not need to sow in spring – so much has already fallen,
implanting itself for next year's display and butterfly feast.
I'll pull out all the giant stalks to make a flat bed
for the blankets of snow coming this winter.

Barbara Shepherd

Posing for a Photograph

Pa, dressed in worn overalls and a comfortable shirt, exhibits extreme patience outside in the dusty street while Mama and I tie ribbons on Sara's pigtails again. We had to wait more than three hours for the old photographer to set up his big camera in the corner of the general store and get the lighting just right.

Mopping sweat from his wrinkled brow and dressed like a dandy, the traveling photographer looks like he's outgrown his best suit of clothes. No wonder people's faces look so drawn, so angry, in their pictures. It's hard work posing for pictures for the better part of a hot afternoon.

Sara sashays around in her new white dress, scratches at her skinny legs in long stockings, and keeps untying her pink satin ribbons. I stand up straight beside Mama to show that I am almost as tall as she. When we get the picture made, I can see how much taller I need to grow to be her same height. My dress makes me itch even though it is made of finely-woven cotton. Mama starched our dresses more than usual yesterday so they would still look good after our trip to town in the long wagon.

She wears a dress of taupe satin, the same one she wore at her wedding and to Grandma's funeral. With her hair piled high on top of her head, Grandma's string of tortoiseshell beads around her tanned neck, and a small, barrel handbag in her hand, Mama looks as stylish as any woman on the street. No one would know she arrived in an old wooden wagon made to carry lumber instead of riding in a fancy carriage, maybe one with fringe on top.

Pa refused to have his picture made and decided to stay outside. Someone needed to keep the mules content anyway. But, they weren't as confused today as usual, so the ride into town went as smooth as fresh-spun linen.

At home, Mama usually drives the lumber wagon while Pa loads slender tree trunks on it from the woods. Although all mules seem to know that "gee" means right and "haw" means left, our mules, Hank and Joe, really have to concentrate on commands. Mama gets them riled up when she says gee but pulls on the reins to get them to turn left. Haw is just as bad. She knows what gee and haw mean, but Mama always intends the opposite. We're used to it. When she says to pass the gravy to the left, she hands the hot bowl to me, sitting on her right. Pa tried to correct her, but after fifteen years, he gave up. She's driven Hank and Joe for half that time, but they still get mixed up with Mama playing mule-skinner.

Now, the photographer says, "I finally have it. Stand real still."

We stand up straight and he says to Mama, "Put your right arm behind Sara and hold your handbag in your left."

Mama says, "Yes, sir." Then, she promptly puts her left arm behind Sara and brings her right one forward with the barrel handbag hanging from the long fingers of her right hand.

Although the photographer's face turns deep red like a ripe beet, I whisper for him to take the picture *now*. He pulls his timepiece from his watch pocket, looks at the late hour, then ducks his head under the camera's canopy and clicks. The small explosion startles us, but he promises us it will be a great picture.

I unfasten Mama's beads and place them in her handbag. When we walk out in the July sunshine, I say, "I've never been so relieved to let the mules take us home."

Barbara Shepherd

Author's Note:
This is a work of fiction inspired by the stern expressions on faces of people, of all ages, in old photographs. Once I discovered they had to sit still for so many hours for photographers to get set up and take that one sepia photo, I could understand the absence of smiles.

Wordwrights OKC Christian Writers
presents:

Michele Simmons

Michele Simmons is slightly self-centered, lost in the fray, lovin' every mad, exhausting minute, and trying to grow up to be a servant-hearted Christian. Your prayers are appreciated. She occasionally blogs at TravelerInMyOwnBackyard.blogspot.com and can be reached at BMRNNP@gmail.com.

Nathan and the Bell Ringers

We pretend it isn't true, but the holiday season can be a grind. Plenty of mundane details, and some days are still ordinary. Until they aren't.

In December, the swanky grocery store in this small town has those red buckets with bell ringers at both entrances. We don't go to the swanky store all the time, just for small things our regular store doesn't carry. Today, I need almonds. Not the roasted almonds, but raw and sliced, so we go to the swanky grocery.

I admit I am getting lost in the hustle, trying to hold onto the reason for the season, but *things* are getting a little overwhelming. Too many places to be, a few too many gift exchanges, a blessedly busy hobby and one kid who has been sick long enough that it nags at the heart of this mom.

Here, there, and everywhere in a glow of Christmas spirit, I decide not to pass the bell ringer with just my smile but wait, let me dig out my change. There is a bunch of it weighing down my purse anyway, right? The kids love putting change in the bucket and maybe if they observe me giving, they will grow up giving too. Yes, I will model giving for my children.

A few days later and that swanky store is right next to the post office which makes it handy. Another friendly bell ringer and I think, glowing warmly inside, I will just try to give something every time we come by. Isn't that a noble goal? Yes, noble goal, and I dig in my purse while surely a mother in some part of the world is watching her cold, hungry kiddo, wishing she had my change.

And another trip or two and the change keeps on coming, handing it out to three happy kids who drop it excitedly into the red bucket while the bell ringer smiles and says, "Merry Christmas! Every little bit helps."

Just now, a friend gives my boy Nathan a Christmas card and two dollars when we stop by the church. He is excited about those two unexpected dollars. We get in the car and ride two minutes to the swanky store. I just have to run in and get milk and bread, you know how it is. As we pull in, we pass the bell ringers, two men chatting by the red bucket. I park, grab my purse and start digging out change. Let's give something each time we go in, remember?

From the back seat comes the uncontainable sound of a joyful voice, "I *know*. I can give them *my* two dollars."

Distracted by trying to dig out quarters, nickels and pennies, I ask, "Are you *sure* you want to do that? I have change that you can give..."

"I can give my two dollars! They need real money too!"

I begin, "Are you..." then something, surely not my own heart, but something, stops me. I fight misty eyes and tell him that would be wonderful. For once, I understand not to steal his joy, and what a beautiful, simple joy it is. I remember words, words about a kingdom for such as these, words about not hindering the children to come to Him.

This boy, who always has a list of Legos that he's saving up for, this boy who has had this found money for less than five minutes, is giving it away because *they* need money, too. And he runs up to the red bucket and stuffs his two dollars in before I can even get there with the other kids. The bell ringers thank him.

But I have a problem, watching this giving joy pour out of him and knowing that boy the way I do, and I am crying in front of the firewood stacked outside the automatic doors. So, I try to explain and I want them to understand because this kid didn't give money from his momma's purse. *He gave his own two mites that he had only two minutes.* *

These two kindly bell ringers see my feelings on my face. They see his pure smile and he's hopping next to the bucket. They pause and try to convey that they know how really big this moment is...and we say goodbye and we go inside.

Milk and bread and life goes on and I am treasuring these things in my heart.

We head out the door and those bell ringers stop us and ask his name. Nathan can't answer. His mouth is full of free sugar cookies from the balloon station. They can't leave their bucket but they have paused their ringing to talk to him, to make an impression on him as he has made an impression on them.

They tell Nathan that he has touched their hearts, giving both of his brand-new dollar bills. These two men, whose hearts are already touched enough to spend an afternoon in the air ringing a bell and watching people like me scoot by the red bucket, tell Nathan that his gift matters.

At home, I call Nathan to me and I ask him if he understands the consequences of his gift. I tell him that his sweet heart and his two dollars blessed me. Then it blessed those men and his own brother and sister who saw it all right there in front of the grocery. We all learned that it isn't even about money but about the heart.

Michele Simmons

Authors note:
To read about the widow who gave her two mites, read Luke 21:1-4.

Christmas Magnificat

(a prayer inspired by Mary's song, Luke 1:46-55)

Father of mine,
Savior,
How is it that you look down on this child?
How can it be that *I* magnify *You*?

You have blessed me.
Bless me again by giving me a servant's soul.
Bless me by growing the seeds that I sow.
Bless me with mercy, welling up like a spring.

You do not bless the strong but the humble.
Give me a humble heart.

You scatter the proud.
Gather me under your wings.

You send the rich away
Fill me with a rich heart.

You keep Your promises.
Keep me, Forever.

Michele Simmons

Dry

It's a dry season here, and I don't mean the weather. I'm like a Christmas tree whose water dried up weeks ago. Still look all right but please, I'm begging you, please, don't shake me.

In my heart it's so dry, I can't think of anything but my parched throat and how bad I want water. Sometimes I don't even care about the cost. Like cattle running to water sweet with too much alkali, only to die from drinking it, my mind runs without reason through all the things I could do that might get me what I think I need.

You ever had a dry season? When it seemed like what you had wasn't enough? Maybe it was money, not enough to go around. Maybe it was love, you get stuck in a rut and it feels like your love is old and tired. Maybe you are tired of wearing a hole in the linoleum at the kitchen sink or the paperwork that doesn't seem to mean anything in this breath we call life. Maybe you are just plain tired after three babies in four years or getting up every morning to go to the same job. Maybe you just need a friend, or a nap. You ever had a dry season like that?

Walking through this desert, my desert, I scan the horizon and see a friend. But I can't cry out to her because she hasn't lived any more than I, and I desperately need someone who has gone before me to show me the path.

Over the next dune, I see another friend, her hair blowing in the wind and I can't cry out to her either because she is too close in and I don't need sweet, alkali words that go down smooth but burn me up inside. I need truth, and maybe she loves me too much to speak it.

Like a mirage, a group of friends appear, 147 of them in fact, but if I am honest with you, I am not sure I trust them. I can't quite go out on a limb with an eFriend whose tears or whose sweat have never mixed with mine.

My heart is dry and cracked and my reason runs wild, failing and fearful but my faith, it is the rock on which I stand.

On solid rock I stand, all other ground is sinking sand, all other ground is sinking sand...

Faith knows the way to the spring. Ha! Faith can walk on water! Faith has strong legs to carry me when my heart and reason fail and most important of all, Faith knows the Way.

Faith knows the Way.

With faith, you can love, even when you feel alone.

With faith, you can find joy, even in the wreckage of life.

With faith, you can wait in peace, even while you pick up the pieces.

Faith knows the way, even when you can't even see the road.

Here's what Faith tells me today, in this dry season along the road called Uncertain. My faith simply says, "Do the next faithful thing. Then do the next one. Another, and another. I, Faith, will lead you. Just do the next faithful thing. One day, when you drink your fill, you will look back and see that you have travelled where you never thought you could."

It's a dry season here, and I don't mean the weather. I'm like a Christmas tree whose water dried up weeks ago. I don't know how I look but you can shake me if you want. I spring – fed by Faith. I am evergreen.

Michele Simmons

All of the Angels

The women sat around the shiny, oak table gathering strength from hot tea, brownies, and each other. The man of the house made himself scarce before the first ring of the doorbell, sent away with promises of treats hidden for him, a sample from each dessert. The boys were greeted, faces pinched, gifted with sweets, and sent upstairs with a whispered threat to keep the noise to a reasonable level.

The women went around the table, led by an organized but reluctant woman with a pixie cut and a sincere heart. They took turns giving a quick update on their lives, kids, interests, and even their struggles. There were gushing compliments about the blueberry-apple crisp, the calories of which could be offset by the recent commercial availability of Stevia to sweeten the tea.

A couple of women cried as they shared their stories. Life is hard sometimes. This circle had only one rule, "If you cry, we pray." The women gathered around the one bowed down by her days and they put their hands out. One pair of hands touched her shoulders, hands worn and cracked by the garden. Manicured nails in Christmas red rested on top of the woman's own hands. Plain hands wearing only a gold band handed her a tissue before they began. They were exquisitely beautiful in that moment.

Across town, the man of the house faced a problem. He drove in the cold, money in his pocket, unsure of where to go to get what he needed. It had to be now, tonight, but he was unaccustomed to dealing with things like this. Being a man of action, he came to a quick decision. He called his wife.

Pixie apologized when the phone rang. The women chatted quietly while she took the call, knowing that her husband might be in some trouble. The one-sided conversation was undeniably puzzling.

"How many? Well, how many angels do you have with you? All of them? You took all of them?"

"Let's see, where would you go? Well, the lingerie department, I think. If they aren't there, you'll have to ask."

"How big? Well, your guess is as good as mine. Maybe you will get lucky and they will be one size fits all. Don't worry, you'll do fine."

Pixie hung up. When she turned, her friends' wide eyes demanded explanation. Normally a no-nonsense kind of woman, Pixie did something unusual. She giggled.

"You must be wondering what that was all about."

The statement hung in the air and Pixie got no help from her friends. Her smile turned from genuine to nervous and she may have squirmed in her farmhouse chair. Pixie offered to make more tea. She offered Stevia.

The silence grew as her friends realized that Pixie didn't want to tell. They were too well-bred to demand an explanation. Then the woman with the red nails remembered that she wasn't too well-bred after all.

"Spill it!" she ordered, "No tea, thank you. I'd like coffee if you have it."

Pixie sighed. There was no escaping them. She was one against the pack and they would have the truth, no matter how sordid, no matter how much she didn't want to tell. And just how do you tell something like this without seeming, well, like you are either bragging or a little crazy?

"It's okay, honey, just tell the whole story. Better to get it out. Why is your husband in the lingerie department?" another friend cooed supportively.

Pixie told the story, about how he was spending his Christmas bonus. They cried again. Then they prayed again, this time with their hands on Pixie.

They were all gone when he pulled in the driveway. He left the goods in the trunk, laid out so they wouldn't wrinkle. He wanted them nice when the elderly women of Autumn Acres finally saw them. It might be the only gift they received this Christmas.

Pixie was curled up on the couch. She could see how happy he was, the joy of giving was, well, it was making her husband glow. It made her happy to see him like this.

"So, what did you end up getting?"

"I don't even know really. By the way, housecoats are in the lingerie department, all off to one side. They come in small, medium and large. The size wasn't really an issue; I bought all of them."

"Was it enough?" Pixie asked, eyebrows raised.

"No, I had to buy three robes to make sure I had one for each old lady, er, angel," he corrected himself respectfully.

"What made you take all the ornaments from the angel tree? I just wondered. It must have been very exciting."

"That's why I love you," he spoke with an unsteady voice. "You are the only woman I can imagine who would be happy to see a Christmas bonus spent on other women. As for the tree, I saw all those angel ornaments up there, and each one had a woman's name on it. I just couldn't stand to think of one of those women, Sarah or Alma or Edith, not getting a housecoat when it was in my hands to give it."

"I love the man that you are and I would go with you anywhere," she whispered.

"That's interesting. How do you feel about the missionary field?" he whispered back.

"Oh my. I'd better get more Stevia," Pixie said in a distracted voice, picturing her friends praying over her again.

In that moment, she was exquisitely beautiful.

Michele Simmons

Shine

Voices say Christmas is about stuff,
we should all just step on out,
refuse to participate.
Not even *really* His birthday.

Children glow in the light of expectation.
They expect what we teach them to expect.
Better to teach them how to see than blindfold their eyes.

Bitter words pour out of the mouths of good people.
"We can't even say 'Merry Christmas' anymore,
they just X Him right out."

The least I can do is say "Merry Christmas."
I say it like a gift of joy and
I will listen to you and we will know each other.
You will know that I am one who believes
And when Spirit shines in your dark,
May I be a beacon to show the Way.

Fuss and family and one more white elephant
They can weigh a soul right down.

Turn weary to worship.
Let go of the weight and the white elephants and
Seek Ye First, Friend,
Seek Him.
He's all that matters anyway.
The rest will be added, see?

Christmas has changed, undeniable.
Shrinking from change won't stop it from comin'
Jesus is the reason,
but maybe
the season is a reason to shine,
the time of year when people *expect* us to speak.
When the lost wait to hear, what will we say?

The light shines in the darkness,
and the darkness did not overcome it.

Don't hide it under a bush, oh no,
I'm gonna let it shine,
Let it shine, let it shine, let it shine...

Michele Simmons

I Am Christmas

I am Christmas
I am pine needles evergreen
Friends, eggnog and nutmeg blowin' right in your front door
Too much money, too much candy, but never too much love.

I am ornaments made of blackjack oak
golden glitter and Beads on a string,
I am the wild wind that sings in your dreams,
Abundance filling your table and your heart.

I am Christmas
The more you give away, the more you have
And brothers and sisters I am NOT talking about presents
But the presence of your heart.

You feel me in your bones
Remember my ancestors and yours
Since time began I have been here
One Way or another, for you.

I am Christmas
You think you can change me?
Maybe I change you!
Maybe you change the world.

I am family you love and sometimes do not like
The kid on the corner who goes home to nothing or worse
I am dusted off memories, held up and put away,
the glory of the past and the promise of the future.

I am Christmas no matter where you are
with the ones you love or alone,
dancing with health, bearing your child or
sitting with one watching the last snow.

I am Christmas
You may NOT pretend I'm not coming!
They pretended that before but
The first time changed everything.

I am every gift you give
every hand you hold
I am every tear you cry
every picture you take.

I am Emmanuel.
I know your name.
I know how to win your heart,
how to hold your hand forever.

I am Christmas
I am Faith
I am Hope
I am Love, come right down to you.

Michele Simmons

Beads to inspire:

Peace

Be anxious for nothing, but in everything by prayer and supplication, with thanksgiving, let your requests be made known to God; and the peace of God, which surpasses all understanding, will guard your hearts and minds through Christ Jesus.

(Philippians 4:6,7 NKJV)

Wordwrights OKC Christian Writers
presents:

Milton Smith

Milton Smith finds that writing is a natural outlet for his creative energy and a means quite similar to photography in capturing life's intriguing, but often fleeting, moments. He is currently working on a historical musical that he hopes will inspire Oklahomans to learn more about the pioneering spirit and human courage that has shaped their state.

Milton can be reached at HisWordMatters@yahoo.com.

A Faithful Friend

God knows we need friends to have a fulfilled life. To me, they are almost always people whom God sent my way, not people I sought to be my friends. One such man, an associate pastor, challenged church members to join him in an early-morning prayer session that met twice a week to pray for the needs of the church.

I accepted the challenge and joined with others to pray. The prayer group enabled spiritual growth. Answers to prayers changed our lives. We rejoiced in church members' healings from diseases and accidents and saw God's grace given to saints who needed help as they passed on from this life. God blessed our church with offerings sorely needed at specific times. Some of our prayers for national concerns we saw answered in newspaper headlines. Personal needs of family members found resolution. We felt like co-workers with God; seeking His will and His glory. Prisoners came to faith in Christ through the witness of men and women who we prayed for specifically. Leaders from youth camps and choir programs reported God's blessings on their efforts. Our personal lives abounded in unexpected blessings at work and in our homes, all due to the prayers of others and the faithfulness of God who hears and answers prayer.

We met for years. I continued to come even after my wife and I changed churches. I found that God is as interested in our personal lives as he is in the various ministries of the church. One time, the associate pastor and I both prayed for our grandsons who played on junior high football teams in different parts of the city. I attended my grandson's game and was impressed when both teams met in the center of the field and huddled for a brief prayer before the game. I had the long-range lens on my camera and took a picture of them praying. About a week later, the associate pastor shared a special experience he had at his grandson's game. His grandson's coach was a Christian man who asked the opposing coach if it would be okay with him if they brought the boys out on the field together for a brief prayer before the game. It was okay with him. The coach then asked the associate pastor if he would give the prayer for the boys. They all met in midfield and my friend led the prayer. He told me it was a great blessing to lead the prayer, especially since his grandson was there. I had to ask him where the game was played and the name of his grandson's team. Sure enough, it was the same game I had attended. I made an enlargement for him of the photo I took. He framed it and later presented it to his grandson's coach. God blessed our grandsons, their coaches, and us in answered prayer.

The last year and a half of our prayer time became a one-on-one experience for the minister and me. For various reasons like job changes, health problems, etc., others dropped out and although the early morning meeting continued to be listed in the weekly church bulletin, no one else joined us for prayer. We enjoyed our time together, not so much because we wanted to talk to each other, but because of our freedom to share our hearts with the Lord and know He listened. Though we struggled to get up early, answered prayer made it all worthwhile. We felt we were a vital part of God's work in the world.

The minister and I lived different lives and rarely saw each other except at the prayer meetings. He developed difficulty in breathing so we postponed our meetings, hoping his problems would be cured. He is with the Lord now. I am grateful for his prayers and friendship and his example. I thank God for bringing such a faithful friend into my life.

Milton Smith

Grandmother's Secret

Sweat Beads on alice's forehead and her struggle to find a position of comfort prompted Ernest to find his heavy coat. Their baby was coming. He had to fetch the doctor.

"Alice, I'll put some water on to boil in the big kettle. Then Molly, she's the fastest of the horses, will get me to Doc's."

"Ernest, just get going. This young one is not waiting."

The journey from his farm on the outside of Omaha, Nebraska, took a good fifteen minutes, thirty for a round trip. Ernest hoped his wife could hold on. He depended on the fence posts to mark his way, since he could not see the snow covered road. Molly seemed unconcerned, enjoying her exercise. None too soon, Ernest and the doctor stomped their boots free of snow on Ernest's front porch.

"Alice, the doctor's here," Ernest said, relieved not to see any blood stains on her bed sheets.

"I am so glad you are here, doctor. I did not want to have this baby on my own. It is ready to come."

"Mrs. Brewster, we came fast as we could through the snow. Ernest, get some towels from my saddle pack."

Ernest retrieved the towels, anything to keep himself busy.

"Thank you Ernest. Would you put a couple of those towels in the kettle of hot water in the kitchen, then bring them to me on a plate. Don't burn your hands."

With two towels in hand, Ernest headed for the kitchen and heard his wife's words to the doctor.

"I do not like having children, doctor, but I guess it is a woman's job."

Ernest had little understanding of birth from a woman's point of view, but it grieved him that his wife did not share the joy of anticipation for a new child. The steaming towels Ernest brought to the doctor were well received.

The doctor wrapped his instruments quickly inside the towels. "Ernest I could use a cup of coffee." The doctor spoke, not missing a beat of his well-rehearsed routine.

Coffee also sounded good to Ernest. He made his way back to the kitchen and poured two cups, one for himself, when he heard Alice scream.

"She is a fine girl, Alice, a fine girl," the doctor said.

Ernest entered the room and saw Alice nod her head in response before she slumped into a sleep of exhaustion. The doctor wiped the child clean, spanking its bottom in the process. No response. He spanked again, nothing. Fear crept into Ernest's heart when he saw the concern in the doctor's face. Vigorous rubbing of the child's body and another spanking brought the same unwelcome result. A cold silence permeated the room. Ernest could hardly breathe, let alone say the word, and he understood why the doctor refused to state the obvious. "Stillborn."

"I am sorry, Ernest. There is nothing more I can do. She is a dear child, a beautiful child, but she is in God's hands now."

Ernest had no words, only tears, as he took the child from the doctor, held her in his arms and walked toward the kitchen. He noticed the small, wooden box on the floor for kindling near the wood stove and quickly dumped its contents. Finding a clean towel, he wrapped the baby in it and placed her in the make-shift crib. A side shelf attached to the stove became its resting place. Ernest returned his attention to the doctor and his exhausted wife.

"Ernest, I'll need some hot water. She is bleeding more than she should, but I believe we can get it stopped."

Ernest went to the kitchen for the hot water and brought it to the doctor. "Is she going to be okay?"

"I believe so, Ernest, but it would not hurt to pray."

Ernest left the bedroom for a private audience with the Lord in the kitchen. Before he addressed the Lord, his quick glance caught movement in the kindling box. Ernest grabbed the box, almost dropping it because of the residual heat from the stove. He pulled the towel- wrapped baby from the box. He blew air into its mouth; another breath and another one. The baby cried. Ernest rushed her to the doctor who turned from his work in surprise.

"God answered our prayers Doc."

Ernest brought the baby to Alice so she could feel and hear this new life. Alice half asleep, lifted her arm to hold her.

"The bleeding has stopped, Ernest. Alice will be all right."

"Thank you, Doctor."

"Thanks be to the Lord, Ernest. It is all His doing," the doctor said.

It was on March 3rd, 1901, that Sara Alice Brewster, later my Grandmother Hogan, came into this world. Although you have read a fictionalized version of that event, the facts of her birth remain as a testimony of God's grace and plan for the family she would have that called her "Mom" and "Grandmother." She was not denied the life God used to be a blessing to so many others. Sara lived to be over one hundred. She was the one unifying factor for her children and grandchildren; remembering each birthday, attending each special event in their lives: graduations, weddings and family gatherings, even when it required traveling long distance at her own expense. Sara's life constantly reflected Christ, in love for her family, love for her church and for missionaries who knew her support in gifts of supplies, bandages, and treats over the years of their service in foreign lands. She also had a deep love for the things of nature, making personal pets of a rock-abused goldfish from her backyard pond and some orphaned opossums.

Sara was married to Glen L. Hogan for 62 years, had four children, sixteen grandchildren, and twenty-one (and counting) great grandchildren. But none of us knew about her near death experience in 1901. She held onto her secret for ninety-five years.

The family had gathered in the basement of the original First Church of the Nazarene in Norman, Oklahoma, to celebrate Grandmother Hogan's ninety-fifth birthday. We learned Grandmother told her story first to Lynn Merie, her youngest granddaughter. Lynn was helping Grandmother brush out her long hair, which Grandmother always kept in a bun. As Lynn combed Grandmother's hair, she noticed a distinctive scar on the back of her head, normally concealed by the bun.

"When did you get that scar, Grandmother?"

"It's an old story. Actually I have two scars. The other one is in the middle of my back. They came from a hot stove when I was born."

After Lynn shared Grandmother's story with us at the party, I looked around at the faces in the basement room: brothers, a sister, cousins, uncles, aunts, nieces, nephews, and my mom, recognizing that if not for the grace of God and my great-grandfather's quick action, none of us would have been present. It was humbling and inspiring. Never again will I believe the words: *What difference will it make a hundred years from now?*

It makes all the difference in the world.

Milton Smith

Beads on a String

Like the beads of a necklace of value untold.
God's blessings sparkle, rare jewels to behold.
Their beauty outstanding, each clear and precise,
To magnify Jesus and His sacrifice.

Stories of joy, rich as rubies, delight,
Poems of love, like diamonds of radiant light,
Songs of peace, pearls He gave in the night,
Testimonies of pure gold, He yearned for someone to write.

Each bead of beauty, each one of a kind,
Designed for a purpose He had in mind.
Each precious jewel put on this string:
Peace, joy, and love – we offer to honor our King.

Milton Smith

A Little Boy's Prayer

Summer thrilled ten-year-old Jimmy; no school, no shoes, no routine. He could do as he pleased. His dad worked, his mom visited over coffee at the neighbors, his older brother Jason played on a baseball team, and his sister Julie entertained herself at her friend's house, playing with dolls.

For Jimmy, the backyard was his favorite place. He could sit for hours staring at clouds. But, as much as he loved his backyard, he needed something more.

One day as his dad finished saying the blessing for supper; it occurred to Jimmy. "I can pray for something fun to do. I'm going to pray for a horse.

Later that night when he knew his brother Jason was fast asleep in the top bunk, he whispered this prayer: "Dear God, I know you hear prayers. I'm just a little boy and I don't have any money, but I want a horse, a small horse, like a pony. Our yard's big enough and I don't think my parents would mind. Please, God, would you send me a horse? I'll take good care of it. Thank you for hearing my prayer."

Jimmy told no one about his prayer. He did let slip, while helping his Mom bake cookies, that he might enjoy having a horse. She said nothing against the idea, so Jimmy kept on reminding God every day – not begging, just reminding God how much he'd enjoy having a horse.

Two months went by, but Jimmy knew God had not forgotten. He almost spilled his tea when his mom asked his dad, "Would you mind calling your brother, Stanley, to see if he has any horses for sale."

"Who needs a horse?" his dad replied.

"My brother, Owen. He recently bought an acreage and his kids want a horse they can ride."

"I'm sure he can find one for them. I'll call him tomorrow."

Jimmy had completely forgotten that his Uncle Stanley bought and sold horses. Not that it made much difference. He lived a hundred miles away! And Jimmy had no money.

The next day, Jimmy's Mom and Dad talked with both his uncles. That evening when the kitchen phone rang, Jimmy picked it up. It was his Uncle Owen. He handed the phone to his mom.

"Yes, Owen. That's good news. But, I'll have to ask my husband about that. Can you hold on?"

Jimmy's mom put her hand over the receiver and said, "Owen and your brother, Stanley, made a deal for the horse. Stanley has to come to the city on business next week and can bring the horse with him. The only problem is Owen hasn't finished putting the fence around his property. He's asking if we could keep the horse in our backyard for a few weeks."

Jimmy, Jason, and Julie shook with excitement.

"There'll be work to do," Dad said as the kids' heads bobbed up and down. "It's ok with me as long as the kids understand they will be expected to help out."

Jimmy's mom returned to her phone conversation. "Owen, tell him to bring the horse. Everyone here loves the idea. You're welcome. See you in a few weeks."

Jimmy, Jason and Julie gave each other high fives, almost knocking dishes off the table.

"Hold your horses," Dad said, laughing at his pun. "Help your mom with the dishes."

Jimmy couldn't sleep that night. He kept thinking: a horse, a horse in my own backyard. Wow! He was expecting a horse but now, he was expecting his horse.

"Dear God, I know you heard me. You know I want my own horse, but thanks for bringing my uncle's horse so I can get used to having one." Jimmy went to sleep, knowing that God was going to work things out. It was just taking longer than he expected.

The next morning, Dad got Jason and Jimmy's attention. "Guys, I was thinking that it would be good to have a corral to keep the horse in. We have plenty of used lumber in that half-opened shed. The shed itself would make a good windbreak. You could build the corral around it. It will take some work, but I believe you two can handle it."

"We'll do it, Dad," Jason said.

The boys spent the morning digging holes for corral posts. Jimmy silently thanked God for the corral that would someday hold his horse. With each hole they dug and each board they nailed, Jimmy became more excited. He wondered what color his horse would be. Jason left for baseball practice so Jimmy took a break too.

"Jimmy," his mom called, "Julie and I are going to the farm store. Want to come along?"

"Sure," Jimmy said without hesitation.

It was a short drive to the farm store.

"We're going to need a bale of hay and some. . . I believe Uncle Stanley said oat mix for horses." Jimmy's Mom didn't know much more about horses than Jimmy, so she also bought a book on raising horses and a cube of salt lick. The store's employees loaded their purchases.

When Jimmy opened the side door of the station wagon for the return trip home, the scent of fresh hay filled his nose and he pictured himself waving a cowboy hat to on-looking neighbors, as he rode his horse from the backyard to the front. The start of the car's engine brought him back to reality, and his sore arms reminded him he still had a corral to finish.

A week later, with corral in place, and food and water buckets ready for use, the anticipated horse trailer arrived. Uncle Stanley, his jovial self, hugged Jimmy's mom, shook Dad's hand, and said "Howdy" to all of the kids. "I have a surprise for you."

"A surprise?" Dad asked.

"Yes sir-ree, how about an extra horse?"

"Extra horse?" everyone echoed.

"Yes, indee dee, she's a nice one. Found her grazing with my other horses. No one in town would claim her, so I brought her along. She's *free.* If you all don't want her, maybe your Uncle Owen would take her."

"I'll take care of her, Mom!" Jimmy shouted. "Dad. Please!" Jimmy could not contain himself.

His dad and mom were beside themselves. They'd never seen Jimmy so ecstatic. Jason and Julie just stood there with their mouths open.

"We'll talk about it, son. Go ahead and help Uncle Stanley get the horses off the trailer."

Jimmy followed his uncle to the trailer.

"Yes sir, Jimmy," said Uncle Stanley, "she'll make you a good riding pony."

Jimmy jumped up and down and wrapped his arms around his uncle, well, almost around him. As Jimmy led the Shetland pony into his backyard behind his uncle and the other horse, he looked up to the sky. He couldn't keep tears from flowing down his face. "Thank you God. I knew you heard me." From that day forward, Jimmy always believed in prayer.

Milton Smith

Author's Note:
Names were changed, but this is a true story. Jimmy named his Shetland pony Sandi after her sand-colored coat of hair.

Beads to inspire:

Joy

These things I have spoken to you, that My joy may remain in you, and that your joy may be full.

(John 15:11 NKJV)

Wordwrights OKC Christian Writers presents:

Connie Sorrell

Connie (Miles) Sorrell was born into a family of writers, editors and publishers. Her great-grandfather, Fred Pruitt, was editor and publisher for Faith Publishing House (FPH) in Guthrie, Oklahoma. Connie's grandmother, Marie, carried on the tradition by writing Sunday school papers for FPH.

Connie has written short stories for the Beautiful Way Sunday School papers and essays for the Faith & Victory newsletter. Over the course of twenty-five years, she wrote and directed Christmas plays and special programs for the Path of Life School where seven of her children attended classes. Currently, Connie has two books carried by Amazon: Our Family's Darlene and A Darlene Summer. She is working on the third book to this sequel, Welcome Darlene. These are fun stories about her youngest daughter who has Down syndrome. Through these stories, she wants to share the love of Jesus, show Darlene's uniqueness, and preserve the memories of her son, Rodney, and her husband, Dwane, who are together in heaven along with her daughter, Vickie.

Following the Dotted Lines

"Grandma, Mama said I can sit by you," my three year old granddaughter said. Her blue eyes twinkled at me as I sat on the red cushion church pew waiting for the service to start.

"Good, Kandis," I said, making room for her beside me and my heavy purse. She climbed onto the pew and snuggled beside me, pulling down her dress printed with blue and pink flowers. In one hand, she had a dry-erase board book that had letters and numbers to copy, and in her other hand, was a blue washable marker and wet wipe.

When the first song of service began, Kandis popped the lid off her marker and proceeded to scribble all over the board book. I saw that she wanted to turn every bit of that page blue, and I knew my task was to prevent any more blue flowers appearing on her dress.

"Here, Kandis, let me help you," I whispered. I quickly wiped the board clean while she frowned as her art work disappeared.

Then my right hand covered her right hand, my bigger fingers interlaced with her smaller ones. We rested the blue marker on her middle finger and pinched it with her thumb and index finger.

"Hold your marker like this," I whispered.

"How come?"

"To write better," I replied. I guided her hand to the dotted U on her board. We followed the arrows and dotted lines, making a big and little U, V, W, X,Y and Z.

After the little z was traced, Kandis giggled. She grabbed the wipe and rubbed off all the marks. Then she looked up at me and said, "Let's do it again, Grandma!"

We held the marker the same way, and while the congregation sang, "I come to the garden alone," we traced letters again. Kandis let my hand guide hers a couple more times. Then at prayer request time, I could feel her fingers and hand pushing the marker along.

"Let's put it away and pray to Jesus," I whispered. She frowned. "We can write later," I whispered.

Right after prayer, she popped the lid off her blue marker. She started down the dotted lines of the W, but her hand wobbled. She quickly wiped off her mark, then looked at me. "Grandma, that was messy," she whispered. "Let's do it again."

I put my right hand over hers and guided her hand down the dotted lines.

By now the pastor, Brother Phillip, was in the pulpit preaching on endurance. Our ears were listening while our hands were writing.

"God has not promised any of us a life of peaches and cream," he said.

Kandis looked up at me and whispered, "We don't have peaches. We have nectarines at our house. Big, fat juicy ones."

"Yes, you're right," I whispered.

"They were so heavy they broke our tree, and we had to pick them before the ants ate them."

"I know," I replied. "We like eating them, don't we?"

She nodded and grabbed up the wipe to clean off the written letters and write them again.

Toward the end of the sermon, Kandis was holding her marker correctly and making readable U's and V's.

The pastor said, "You can be like Saul and kick against the Lord if you want to, but He has good plans for your life if you will let Him guide you through the hard times."

Kandis looked up at me in alarm. "No, you're not supposed to kick," she said firmly. "Mama said not to ever kick anyone. It is naughty to kick."

"Sh-sh, Kandis," I whispered as my left arm drew her close to me. "He said it was wrong to kick…"

Kandis turned around in my arm so she could see me. "He said, *you can kick if you want to!* And that is naughty!"

A few people were looking at us by now. *Oh, no!* I thought. *We are ruining our good behavior record in church!*

"Sh-sh, Honey," I whispered. "If you want, we can ask him after church what he said."

Her face relaxed into a smile and she nodded. She settled down to wipe her board clean. Right after church, we rushed to the rest room and made blue water in the sink as we washed our hands clean.

Hand in hand we walked out of the ladies room. "Now let's find Brother Phillip and ask him what he said about kicking," I said to Kandis.

"No, I don't want to," she replied, shaking her head.

"Don't you want to ask him if it is naughty to kick?" I patted her soft, fawn-brown hair and side braid.

Her blue eyes twinkled up at me, "That's Victor's grandpa and he tells Victor not to kick."

Victor is a cousin a year younger than she.

"Oh, I see," I said.

In her important voice, Kandis added, "You know, Grandma, it is naughty to kick."

"Yes, it is, Kandis," I replied. "And you were a very good girl in church."

We hugged before she skipped away to play with Victor and her little brother, Kurtis.

In my mind I prayed, "Lord, help me to not kick against You, but put your hand over me and guide me over the dotted lines you have made for my life.

Connie Sorrell

Higher-Up Prayer

Oh, Lord, You know my heart's desire
In moving on and climbing higher
Above dark fears that weight my feet
And try to hold me in defeat.

Despite the pain of human woe
I feel about me here below
Give me direction by your grace
And lift me up in Your embrace.

On wings of Truth, let me soar.
And endless heights, let me explore.
High in Your love, I see promises
Sealed with Your rainbow kiss.

So daily, give me strength to rise
Into faith's eternal skies;
Let the clouds of trustworthy white
Surround my mind in peaceful flight.

Light my thoughts with revelation
With the Son shine of expectation
That I may uphold Your Word
And trust you more, my Lord.
Amen.

Connie Sorrell

Upon a Bed
(The End of June)

I sighed in pain as I lay on my lonesome bed. Another June 20th had passed, marking thirty years since we said good-bye to our oldest daughter, Vickie.

"Oh, my throbbing head," I moaned. I put a lightweight pillow over the top of my head but it did not stop the flow of memories.

I kissed Vickie's forehead. She was warm. Her eyelids closed. Her breath stopped. I stood up with the extra weight of a baby soon to be born. I leaned my head on my husband's shoulder and I felt Dwane's arms around me. His body shook with sobs and his hot tears fell on my head. God stopped my sobs for the unborn baby's sake.

Sharp pains hit my stomach, but I did not want to get up to empty it, so I lay still, remembering what happened eight days later, June 28th.

I held a damp, newborn son in my arms. He snuggled close for his first nursing. My fingers touched his soft cheeks that sucked in and out as he drank. My husband was on the phone, talking to his mother. "Connie just had a baby boy! The midwife didn't make it here in time so I delivered him! All went well—she had a short labor after all the stress she has been under—I am thankful! Yal, the midwife is on her way. She needs to weigh him and take care of all the after things.

I reached up and pulled the pillow over my head and around my ears. "It's okay to hear the excitement over Rodney's birth," I said to myself. I took a deep breath to calm my shaking as I recalled that bittersweet night.

"Oh, he's a handsome little boy,? the pastor's wife said as she took Rodney in her arms. "Let me clean him and put some clothes on him. Can I do that?"

I nodded in relief. The pastor and his wife made it to our house before the midwife. She retold this story many times later about putting Rodney's first clothes on him.

When the midwife arrived, she took his clothes off to weigh him in her sack scale. 'Seven pounds, eleven ounces!' she announced. 'He is a healthy, bouncing baby boy! Now, Mama, let's see about you!'

I moaned and rolled over in bed, the same bed where Rodney had been born. In fact, this bed has been with me since I bought it with my work money before I was married 36 years ago. I shook two pillows and tried to make them hug my aching shoulders. My thoughts flew back over the years.

As the scripture says, I soon forgot all the pains of childbirth in rejoicing that a man child was born. His first year of life is a blur in my mind but I know I held him most of the time. We missed our Victory-in-Jesus (as I called Vickie) but Rodney was a comforting "sonshine" who smiled easily.

Two years later, Kevin was born on this bed. A few months later, so were Gerald and a few years later, Darlene. Dwane and I were blessed with four sons and four daughters!

My eyelids squeezed tightly as I felt hot tears trail down the temples of my face, recalling how God dealt with me before he took Rodney away. It was the last of June. Rodney was getting weaker from cancer. I was fighting in my mind for his life.

Please, God, take me instead! Please do not take Rodney! He is such a soul winner for you—please, leave him here to work for you—please!

I love Rodney more than you do, the Lord said. Please trust my wisdom in this decision.

Why? Why are you taking him from me! I demanded an answer. God's silence made me angry, but not Rodney. He showed us all how to have faith in Jesus for the final crossing we all will make some day. It didn't seem fair to me to say good-bye to him on his twenty-fifth birthday, but he was looking forward to his first birthday in heaven, if it could be called such.

With the edge of the top sheet, I wiped away my tears. By now my physical heart was hurting. I groaned. Sharp pains were shooting down my left arm. I bent my arm back and forth to relieve the tension, but the pain increased. Dwane never fully recovered from Rodney's passing. I remembered the following winter.

Dwane lay on the bed, moaning with pain. I rubbed the top of his head and cooled his forehead with a cloth.

"Call the pastor for prayer," he said.

Soon the pastor and five men of God were in our bedroom. After words of encouragement, prayers were said.

Dwane relaxed and went to sleep. The men left.

The pains in my chest and arm intensified. I fluffed up pillows and sat up more in the bed so I could breathe better, but the pain continued with the memories. Five winters later, Dwane lay on this bed, his breathing labored.

I kissed his sweaty brow, but he could not kiss me back. I patted his puffing cheeks, rubbed his legs and feet, and held his stiffening hand. It was a cold February morning when he left me and his earthly family to join his heavenly family. I sobbed because I couldn't keep him here.

My heart was hurting so badly that I thought, "Maybe I will just have a heart attack and join them in Heaven!"

The thought of seeing Dwane, Vickie, Rodney and all my other loved ones in Heaven released a joy in my soul. I felt a warm, soothing oil of healing flow through my body.

"Heaven is just a few short breaths away," I told myself. "My loved ones in Heaven aren't that far away."

My left arm relaxed and my heart stopped hurting. My stomach pains left and my nerves loosened. With thoughts of Heaven floating in my head, I drifted off to sleep. Jesus will take me to see them when He is ready, but it wasn't that night.

Connie Sorrell

My Baseball Victory
(Written for a son)

I hit the ball and sent it flying
Then 'round the bases my legs flew
Right to home plate I was running
With the ball in hot pursuit.

Slam! Bam! We hit home plate together
Which caused both teams to holler:
"He is safe!" I heard my team shout.
"The ball was first, and he is out!"

Replied the other team; and soon
An awful argument broke loose,
Enough to send us all to doom
And I myself felt like a goose.

'Cause no one questioned me at all:
"Who was first—you or the ball?"
At last, someone thought to ask me.
"The ball was first," I said, truthfully.

Well, I was out; we lost the game,
But truth brings victory within.
On its side, there is no shame,
So truth and I, we won again.

Connie Sorrell

The Churn of Life at Our House

After my husband's passing this winter, I was going through many papers when I came across this story I had written about Darlene who was six years old at the time. I chuckled. Darlene may be considered slow due to Down Syndrome, but she has kept her family busy from day one. Here is the story I found:

"Mama, I help?" Darlene asked me as she slipped down from the kitchen chair and took the blue dustpan from my hand. Kneeling, she tilted the dustpan as I had shown her to do. I swept most of the dirt into the pan and she moved it backward a little to receive the rest.

"Thank you, Darlene!" I exclaimed. "You did a wonderful job!"

"Thank you!" she repeated with a happy smile on her face. Carefully, we walked together to the trash can and dumped the dirt. Then we kissed each other's cheeks to celebrate our great teamwork.

"Oh, my darling daughter," I thought as I continued to sweep our cream-colored ceramic tile. "Why do I get so aggravated at you sometimes?"

Then as I pushed the broom under the kitchen table and its long tablecloth, I recalled a scene from a few evenings ago:

Darlene had met me at the front door when I came in from the grocery store with my arms full of groceries.

"Mama! Mama!" she exclaimed, running to me with her arms outstretched. She hugged my legs all the way to the kitchen before I could free my arms for our embrace.

"Mama at work?"

"Yes, I was at work first. Then I went shopping and I thought of you a lot!" Her happy grin conveyed that she was pleased to know that.

As we walked back through the living room, Darlene said, "Sh-sh! Quiet! Daddy sleepin'!"

Sure enough – Babysitter Number One was snoozing soundly on the couch.

"Need help?" Darlene asked me when I opened the front door to go outside.

"Yes, I will hand you something to carry. Stay by the door," I told her.

That's when Babysitter Number Two appeared on the scene. "Mom, am I glad to see you!" exclaimed Lyndall, my oldest son. He walked out to the car with me to help carry in groceries.

"Darlene squished a banana all over the floor, and when I made her clean it up, she just cried *Mama! Mama!* like wiping with a wet cloth was killing her. After we cleaned up the banana mess, I turned around and she was pulling the tape out of a cassette cartridge! I took the cassette from her and while I was reeling in the tape, she went to get a screwdriver, saying she wanted to help, but she pulled the junk drawer all the way out, and stuff fell all over the floor!"

"I am sorry, Lyndall," I said. "Believe me, I know how busy Darlene is and I appreciate you watching her. If we can only channel her busyness into usefulness, then we will be on the upward climb in her training."

Darlene was at the doorway waiting for her share to carry. Quickly, I grabbed a box of butter sticks and handed them to her "Here, Darlene, carry this to the kitchen."

"All right!" she said happily and followed us into the kitchen. While I put away groceries, Lyndall checked out his repaired tape in the nearby cassette player.

After a while I looked around the kitchen, then asked Lyndall, "Where is Darlene?"

He shrugged and looked around the kitchen. Then he looked under the tablecloth.

"Oh, no, Mom, you aren't going to like what she is doing," he said.

"What has she done now?" I peeked underneath the cloth. Darlene was kneeling. Her right hand held a square stick of butter and she was scribbling with it all over the floor and chair legs.

I pulled out a chair and sat down, exhausted. Lyndall had enough energy to guide her out from under the table without her slipping.

"Okay, little gal, the floor is not better with Blue Bonnet on it!" he informed her.

Her blue eyes looked worried as I took the dripping slice of butter from her greasy hand. I took a deep breath. Lyndall disappeared into his bedroom with the cassette player. Darlene tried to hug me, but I prevented the oily encounter. She started to cry.

"Darlene," I said as calmly as I could, "how many times have I told you not to write on the floor?"

She nodded.

"Remember how you had to wash that green marker stuff off the floor?"

She nodded.

"It took a long time, didn't it?"

She nodded.

"So did the blue crayon that you tried to erase with your brother's eraser. You ruined an eraser. The floor still has faint green and blue marks from those times. Why did you do so much scribbling with a stick of butter of all things!?"

Darlene shrugged. Then she glanced under the tablecloth. "No show," she explained. She was right – the yellow butter did not show color on the cream-colored tiles.

"Then never, ever do this again!" I exclaimed.

She nodded. "Never, Mama, never! No show!"

I smiled in spite of myself. Then with warm cloths, we cleaned up the oil slick before it spread.

We were finished cleaning and Darlene was putting away some canned goods when Babysitter Number One walked into the kitchen. Darlene ran to her daddy with her arms outstretched.

He swung her up into his arms. "How is Daddy's Little Sugar!" he said. "Helping Mama, I see."

Darlene nodded and hugged her daddy's neck.

He turned to me and said, "She has been such a good little girl while you were gone, Honey. We went to sleep on the couch together while I was reading her a book. She is really learning to be quiet and good."

I stood still and watched them kiss each other's cheeks. Why should I spoil their happiness with a report of naughtiness? Everything was cleaned up and life seemed as smooth as butter, so the tablecloth and I agreed to keep the written butter message under cover.

Swish! Swish! My broom gathered another pile.

"Here, Darlene, bring the dustpan – I have some more dirt for it," I called.

"All right!" she exclaimed happily. She adjusted the dustpan and I swept the dirt into it. Together we carried it to the trash can, dumped it, and kissed over our good teamwork.

As I drew Darlene close to me, her little eyes sparkled with pleasure that I liked her help.

"Oh, Lord Jesus," I prayed. "Help me to have patience and wisdom to teach this precious little darling that she will be a worker for You and a blessing to others."

As I read over this story written ten years ago, I realized Darlene has grown in obeying – she only writes on paper – and her drawings and love notes to her family and others are received as blessings.

Connie Sorrell

Wordwrights OKC Christian Writers
presents:

Kathryn Spurgeon

Kathryn Spurgeon has published over 100 articles, devotionals and poems. Her work has appeared in publications such as the *Lutheran Digest, Thanking the Troops, Moore Newspaper, Hearts of Hope, Voices in Time* and the *Daily Oklahoman.* She has won numerous writing awards and has been the Writing Team Leader of Henderson Hills Baptist Church, which has published seven devotionals and/or books of faith. She holds a bachelor's degree from OU and has pursued Creative Writing at the University of Central Oklahoma. She is a retired CPA. Kathryn and her husband, Bill, have six children and twelve grandchildren.

Blue Feather

A blue feather floated
to the ground today.
I chased it over the pasture.
It circled, evading
my clutch and my grasp,
Then laughed and went even faster.

"Now, I don't believe
you can catch me," he said.
"The wind is bigger than you."
So he danced and began
the jitterbug fling
and I didn't know what to do.

The blue feather mocked
and flew through the trees.
He giggled way up to the clouds.
Over the fence
and around the pond,
he startled my daddy's milk cow.

Now I'll wait and be patient,
for I know some day
he must return to his senses,
and allow me to make
a blue feather hat
and pretend I'm an Indian princess!

Kathryn Spurgeon

Glass Memories

My life a glass bottle
dead flowers of memories
remnants of joy
traces of tears
no longer the blossoms
my heart held dear,
bits of sunshine
when life grew to be
beautiful, warming,
light and carefree
beyond the roses
faded from view,
days when my fortune
began to come true.

Kathryn Spurgeon

Anger, Go Away

I once left Anger on my covered front porch.
He knocked at my door but I feared getting scorched.

I refused to answer; ignored him for days.
I hoped and prayed he would run far away.

But my Fear Dog told him to pout and to cry.
I looked through my window and heard this reply,

"I live here, too. You must let me in!"
But I screamed, "Don't be silly. You're only my sin!

I don't want you here. Peace lives in your room.
I like him better. Don't bring me your doom."

Fear Dog told him to never give up.
Anger pouted and cried, "That's enough!"

He banged and the door began to cave through.
Then Faith took my hand, said, "This isn't new."

Patience stepped forward. Ah, my team, my support.
"We're in this together. Don't give a retort.

What's a few broken windows, graffiti, and all.
Don't worry, Anger will grow tired and stall."

And sure enough, soon, Anger stomped as he went.
He loped through the yard, jumped over the fence.

May he never look back. If he does, I'll just say,
"You're not welcome here. Love has moved in to stay."

Kathryn Spurgeon

Like a Fountain

How can God love me this much
when my past is flawed and dirty,
when my faults bring filth and scorn?
When my head hangs low in disgrace
and my mind sees only thorns?

Can the mountains cry "He's bigger?"
Can the mouse squeak, "Him I see?"
Is He monstrous huge or minuscule
or somewhere in between?

Can His love be therapeutic?
Bring new health to weary bones?
Will He help me when I'm tortured?
Can He hear my silent moans?

God's love gushes like a fountain,
flows from depths I cannot see.
I may never comprehend it,
but I gulp and I am free.

Kathryn Spurgeon

Wordwrights OKC Christian Writers
presents:

Jean Stover

Jean Stover is a retired teacher and speaker who writes fiction, non-fiction, and poetry. During her 28 years as a public school teacher, she helped students write poetry, short stories, and family histories.

Jean has published two chapbooks of poetry and has written two books: To God Be the Glory and Sirloin Stockade Slaughter.

Recently, she enjoyed her role in the movie, *Skid*, which was filmed in Oklahoma.

Resurrection

For a week the Jews followed Jesus,
Loud hosannas filled the sky.
Then, just days later,
Fickle crowds called, "Crucify!"

Eleven confused disciples
Ran quickly from the cross
To find a hiding place
Where they mourned their loss.

Women came early that first day
To anoint His body with myrrh,
But they found an angel there
Who said, "He is not here."

They took the news to His disciples
Who came together to pray,
Rejoice and greet Jesus,
On that glorious day.

The men became a marching army.
Through the ages, their voices ring,
"Come and meet our Savior.
He is Lord of Lords, and King of Kings."

Jean Stover

Smile

Put a happy thought in your heart
And put a smile on your face.
Lift your head as you impart
What you know to be God's grace.

Turn that frown upside down
As you go from place to place.
In the country or the town
Put a smile on your face.

You may lift another's sorrow,
Perhaps their problems you'll erase.
Troubles, you don't need to borrow,
So keep a smile on your face.

Jean Stover

Wordwrights OKC Christian Writers
presents:

Norman Styers

Norman Styers earned his Ph.D. in religious studies from Boston University. He also has an MA in English from UT-Permian Basin, and did his undergraduate work at Southern Nazarene University in Bethany, Oklahoma.

A former journalist and teacher, he has released four books: Chess Devotionals, First Verses, Deconstruction for Linear Thinkers, and The Legend of Abner and Other Funny Poems. He has contributed poetry, papers, and articles to a variety of books and periodicals.

A native Oklahoman, he lives in Oklahoma City with his wife and three children.

The Faith of William Oakchiah

I grew up in an area where Christianity was once an outlawed religion: not some exotic foreign locale, but Creek County, Oklahoma.

In 1836, the Creek Nation banned the Christian religion within its borders. They expelled the missionaries who lived among them and closed their schools. During this time of persecution, the courage of a young Choctaw man named William Oakchiah helped to keep the worship of God alive.

The Creeks were reacting to the extremely unjust treatment they had received at the hands of the American government. In the 1820's and 1830's, they and other tribes were forcibly removed from their ancestral lands in the southeastern United States and relocated to the Indian Territory, which is now Oklahoma. The hardships and deaths suffered by the Creeks, the Cherokees, the Choctaws, the Chickasaws, and the Seminoles were staggering.

Before the removals, Christian missionaries had made great progress towards converting these nations to faith in Jesus. But even many of the missionaries supported the removal, arguing that the Indians would be easier to convert away from the corrupting influence of the white man. The Presbyterians have the honor of being the only major Christian group officially to oppose the removal of the tribes from their lands and possessions; the Quakers also deserve an honorable mention in this regard.

The cruelty of the removals destroyed most of the progress the missionaries had made. The horrible injustices inflicted on the tribes caused most of them to resent anything to do with the white government, or with Christianity, which was viewed as the white man's religion.

The level of hostility varied from tribe to tribe. The Cherokees, many of whose leaders were Methodists, remained at least officially friendly to missionary work.

The Creeks, a proud people who clung tenaciously to their ancient ways, were the most bitterly opposed to Christianity. They made the worship of the Christian God punishable by 50 lashes on the bare back. The punishment for a second offense was another 50 lashes and the removal of an ear.

Throughout the territory, it became dangerous for a tribal member to profess faith in Jesus. The example of the Creeks helped make the opponents of Christianity in the other nations bold to attack believers.

I never knew as I was growing up in eastern Oklahoma on what had been Creek lands that Christianity had once been outlawed there. But one can hardly blame the tribes. The church had said nothing when the United States government robbed them of their lands, their homes, their possessions, and often their lives. In some cases, the churches even gave the government their cooperation.

Today missionaries acknowledge the difference between a cultural issue and a religious issue, and do not try to separate converts from their cultural identity unnecessarily. But in the nineteenth century, missionaries often attacked tribal customs, not because they were un-Christian, but simply because they were unfamiliar to them.

And yet in the midst of all this ill-treatment, the Gospel continued to touch hearts. And although many records were lost in those turbulent times, and in the even greater unrest of the American Civil War, one story has come down to us of a young man who kept the faith.

William Oakchiah was a member of the Choctaw tribe. We do not know how he became a Christian. The most likely guess is that he studied at a mission school and learned about Jesus there, or perhaps he was brought to Christ by a friend.

He certainly didn't come to faith through his family, for his father, in a dramatic gesture, drew a gun, pointed it at his chest, and ordered his son to give up the white religion. Oakchiah drew himself up to his full height, bared his chest, and said: "Shoot, father, but I will not forsake my Lord."

His father, when he saw the depth of his son's commitment to Christ, dropped the gun and embraced him. He later became a Christian himself.

This story was widely circulated among the other Christians in the Indian Territory. Although some were punished for their belief in Jesus, it is said that none of them gave up their faith because of the persecution, and that the example of William Oakchiah helped them remain true to Christ.

Little more is preserved about this courageous man. We know that he ministered in two Methodist churches for a year in 1844, after the ban against the Christian faith had been lifted. Because he seems to have served only for one year, he was probably supplying the pulpits as a lay preacher. The tribal cultures placed high value on personal courage, so even non-Christians held Oakchiah in respect. He died in a friend's house after collapsing on the street in Fort Smith, Arkansas, penniless but with great honor.

Remaining loyal to Christ can be difficult in any time, but the example of William Oakchiah can inspire us to face those challenges confidently. Few have remained so faithful in the face of so many obstacles. His story should not be forgotten.

Norman Styers

Pendulum

My two-year-old sits under a swing,
Shoves it away; it comes back to hit her.
She's angry now, pushes harder, adds force
To its return. Determination can't win
This battle: the harder she tries to be rid
Of it, the harder it attacks her:
The sin that so easily besets us,
The gravity well of the human soul.

Norman Styers

Faith and Hope

Most of us often think of hope as faith in a weakened form. Our everyday speech makes that easy for us. Where faith expresses a certainty, hope expresses only a probability, or only a possibility.

Suppose a family member asks a doctor, "Was the surgery in time?" and the doctor says, "I believe so." The family will understand that the doctor is expressing confidence that the patient will regain health. But if the doctor says "I hope so," the family will take that to mean that perhaps the operation was in time, but perhaps not. In that situation, any of us would rather hear "I believe so" than "I hope so."

Yet the Scriptures speak as though hope were as important as faith, and certainly as more than simply a positive attitude. Nothing is wrong with using these words in an ordinary way, but we should try to gain the deeper understanding that the Bible offers. If hope were nothing more than a weak form of faith, why would Paul rank it with faith and love?

In a case like this, a Christian from another era can help us look past the way we talk. Saint Augustine, one of the wisest leaders God has given us, spoke a different language, and in many ways thought differently than we do. He can show us a way around the limitations of our own outlook. He describes the difference between faith and hope in this way:

> But hope has for its object only what is good, only what is future, and only what affects the man who entertains the hope. For these reasons, then, faith must be distinguished from hope, not merely as a matter of verbal propriety, but because they are essentially different. The fact that we do not see either what we believe or what we hope for, is all that is common to faith and hope.

Augustine acknowledges one important similarity between faith and hope. Both can be considered a kind of seeing. One of the most famous descriptions of faith in the Bible is that it is "the evidence of things not seen" (Hebrews 13:1). And Paul, speaking of hope, asks: "Hope that is seen is not hope. Who hopes for what he sees?" (Romans 8:24)

The first difference that Augustine points out is that hope directs itself toward the good, but faith can be directed toward something that is not good. That may seem an odd statement, but he explains that we may, for instance, have faith that the wicked will be eternally punished. We do not hope for this to happen. We hope they repent, just as God seeks the repentance of each person.

In a similar way, we may hope to win a magazine sweepstakes (a good thing) even though we know that this is extremely unlikely. But on the other hand, no one hopes to be struck by a meteor, even though that is also extremely unlikely.

Second, hope looks only towards the future, but faith may look either to the past or to the future. So we have faith in the death of Christ (a past event) and the return of Christ (a future event), but we hope in his return.

Finally, hope always involves the person who has the hope. Faith can be directed either to our own good or to the good of others, but hope involves the good of the person who hopes. This does not mean that hope is somehow selfish. But when we say we hope that our children will be accomplished and successful, we have hope because they are our children. We might hope for some other person's success also--it would certainly be churlish to want someone to fail just because we don't happen to be acquainted with them--but the further away the person is from us, the more abstract and less lively the hope is apt to be.

Two examples from the Bible may make this clearer. Shadrach, Meschach and Abednego exhibited both faith and hope when they refused to bow down to the idol of the king (Daniel 3). They expressed their faith in God and their confidence that God was able to deliver them from whatever punishment the king might devise. But they added: even if God does not deliver us, we will not bow down. Their faith in God made them sure that God could do anything he wanted, including saving their physical lives. Their hope was that God would act to save them in their particular circumstances--something that was good, future, and quite thoroughly involved them. But whatever the outcome of their hope, they kept their faith in God, and acted in obedience to God.

God, in response to our faith, may indeed heal a loved one, but our faith is faith in God, not faith in healing, or faith in faith. We must keep on moving toward God in faith, even if our hopes are not fulfilled. If we become angry with God for his failure to obey us, we have made an object of hope an object of faith, and are endangering our relationship to God.

The Resurrection is another example of something in which we have both faith and hope. For our loved ones, we have the hope of the resurrection. When they die, it means that God has not acted to banish death from them--yet. We nevertheless have faith that eventually he will act in the world to destroy death, not only in the individual cases that we care about for our own personal reasons, but for all of us. We can and should hope for God to act, but whether he does or not, we must not bow down to the idol.

The resurrection faith focuses on the God who can raise the dead and who has raised our Lord as the firstfruits, the precursor of our own resurrection. The resurrection hope applies this faith in what God will do to our loved ones who have gone on before us. Resurrection hope is not a weak form of resurrection faith, nor does it suggest that we consider the event hoped for any less likely.

"Hope does not disappoint," Paul tells us (Romans 5:5). Whatever the outcome in worldly terms, hope is rooted in faith, for unless we are moving toward God we have no hope in the world. In the light of our faith we see that, whatever may result in the short run (and in God's view the "short run" may be a very long time), ultimately the Judge of all the world will do right.

Norman Styers

No Exit

I know I should get off and turn around
But that last exit wasn't marked so well,
And the one before, I couldn't change lanes.
I know I should get off and turn around
But hey, you know, it's like that old joke says,
I may be lost but I'm making great time.
I know I should get off and turn around
But this exit has no nice place to eat,
And the oncoming cars merge from the left.
I know I should get off and turn around
Somewhere, sometime soon, before I change states.

Norman Styers

Too Spiritual

I know someone more spiritual than Christ.
Lucifer wears no encumbering flesh:
He, a shadowy Hegelian *Geist*,
Has no rhythms to check his wickedness,
No simple needs to teach humility,
No contented fullness to curb his greed.

Angels don't suffice to satisfy me,
Mystic forces bore me silly, I need
No ghostly deity: Give me a God
Who deals in fire, oil, stones, water, bread, blood.

Norman Styers

A Complaint from My Lawn

You poets, you're always going on about us –
    Leaves of grass!
    Celebrate uniqueness!
    Treasure individuality!
Doesn't keep you from mowing, though.

Norman Styers

Wordwrights OKC Christian Writers
presents:

Lori Williams

A former columnist for MetroFamily Magazine and a current interviewer/writer for the Oklahoma Venture Forum ezine, Lori Williams most enjoys recounting stories of God's grace in everyday circumstances. When she isn't writing about cantaloupe moons or pink flamingo sunsets, Lori enjoys scrapbooking, gardening, and baking homemade bread.
She lives with her handsome husband and delightful daughter in Bethany, Oklahoma.
She can be reached at: dewlaw@cox.net.

Sovereign Wings

"Am I only a God nearby," declares the Lord, "and not a God far away? Who can hide in secret places so that I cannot see them?" declares the Lord. "Do not I fill heaven and earth?" declares the Lord. (Jeremiah 23:23-24 NIV)

Clyde soars over six of seven continents until his homing instinct draws him back to familial nesting sites. Peregrine falcons may fly 15,000 miles a year in search of the perfect aerie.

Before settling down in Oklahoma, Clyde spent summers in his tundra kingdom and winters on his skyscraper throne. But on a recent flight from the Arctic to South America, he stooped to catch a pigeon and landed in the hands of a falconer. Now, he flies for sport and comes home to the suburbs. The bars on his chest mimic the pattern of his days, yet his purpose is a sacred one.

"Do not I fill heaven and earth?" the Lord asks. The world overflows with all of God and all that is his, from a splash of ocean water to the tumble of granite on Mount Scott. Those smudges on Clyde's wings are camouflage. That yearning in my heart is for a closer walk with the Lord of all creation.

"Who can hide in secret places so that I cannot see them?" the Lord asks. Clyde's rapier-like beak and quilted stockings aren't accidental accoutrements: *Peregrīnus* means beyond the borders of the field. Clyde pushes those limits by finding habitation everywhere except Antarctica. Though less hardy, I'm apt to seek out a more scenic route, a more entertaining venue, or a more profitable enterprise. But, there is no migrating from God's love.

"Am I only a God nearby," the Lord asks, "and not a God far away?" This is the greatest comfort of all, for the Creator of time and space is constrained by neither one. God listens to the prayers of my 80-year-old mother who lives in Texas. He hears my petitions as I live and work in Oklahoma. He is attuned to the supplications of my missionary friend in Indonesia who is on her knees twelve hours ahead of me. God is the Alpha and the Omega who is and who was and who is to come. (Revelation 1:8) That 180-degree swivel of Clyde's neck is a reminder that God never shifts his gaze away from me.

The God of the far-away is not a distant God. He is the God watching over my special needs daughter when I am no longer here. (Matthew 28:20) He is the God preparing a heavenly aerie for me. (John 14:3) He is the God who is the same yesterday, today, and forever. (Hebrews 13:8)

Lori Williams

The CloudBlazer

And the LORD went before them by day in a pillar of cloud to lead the way, and by night in a pillar of fire to give them light, so as to go by day and night. He did not take away the pillar of cloud by day or the pillar of fire by night from before the people. (Exodus 13:21-22 NIV)

Though a small thing to most, this trip was a behemoth to me. "God, please lead the way," I prayed while I downloaded directions from Google Maps. My daughter Aurelia wanted to attend a weekend camp in Shawnee while my husband needed to be 80 miles away at a ministry event in the Arbuckle Mountains. The interstate was the shortest distance between home and camp, but I don't do four lane highways. So Aurelia and I were taking the back roads.

This was roll-down-your-window territory, with its country counterpoint of baled hay and red-winged blackbirds. I was grateful for the fresh air after passing through NE 36th and its towering East Oak Landfill, gilded Buddhist statuary, and dead end at Triple X Road. My daughter sat beside me, content to read and push the buttons on the cassette deck in our Dodge pickup.

The long stretches of smooth asphalt meandering through cattle country soothed my nerves until a road sign announced an upcoming intersection. Where was that turn? Would that semi-truck behind me please give me some space?

Then the white TrailBlazer ahead of me slowed and eased into the Highway 62 turn lane. I followed, grateful for my own personal CloudBlazer.

In referring to the literal presence of God going before the children of Israel in the wilderness, Matthew Henry wrote: "The wind could not scatter this cloud."[1] Were the storms stifled during all those 40 years of traveling so that the cloud would move unperturbed ahead of the throng? Or was this cloud unfazed by the gusts blowing through the camp? My focus is often blurred by doubts swirling through my head, but they don't alter the One who goes before me.

Even though I didn't envision a tangible presence leading me when I prayed for guidance, God didn't downsize his provision for me. In fact, at another tricky transition, a different vehicle led the way. That happened in Shawnee, but I had already come safely through Forest Park, Harrah, and Choctaw – plus that other spot on the map I'll never forget: the city of McLoud.

[1]Henry, M. (1706). Exodus. In *Matthew Henry commentary on the whole Bible (complete).* Retrieved from http://www.biblestudytools.com/commentaries/matthew-henry-complete/exodus/

Lori Williams

Wordwrights OKC Christian Writers
presents:

Dorothy Palmer Young

Dorothy Palmer Young was raised in Baltimore, Maryland, but now calls Edmond, Oklahoma, home. She writes devotionals and personal experience stories for her church and other publications. Her story *Time Flies* is included in Chicken Soup for the Caregiver's Soul.

Dorothy and her husband have four children and three grandchildren.

You may contact her at dorothypalmeryoung@cox.net.

A Special Christmas Visit

There is magic at Christmas, so like any other preschooler, I impatiently waited for that special day.

My brothers and I and our parents had moved 800 miles away from the family in Atlanta. We were happy in Baltimore, but so far away from everyone, the only visitor we could expect this Christmas Eve would be a cheerful and pudgy, bearded old guy in a red suit and black boots.

Since we had no chimney, Santa would have to come in through the front door. Too bad he wouldn't show up until I was asleep – I really wanted to see him!

At 6:30, there was a knock at the door. Had Santa come *before* bedtime after all?

Daddy opened the door. Peeking around him, I saw a tall, skinny, clean-shaven, young man wearing a black coat and dark blue pants, with a bag slung over his shoulder. Hey, that wasn't how Santa Claus dressed.

"Merry Christmas," he called in a hearty, southern voice.

Mommy hurried into the room. "David," she squealed. "What are you doing here?"

"Well, Sis," my Uncle David said, beaming. "The Navy gave me a one-day pass, so I came up from Norfolk to see you. Got room for one more for Christmas?"

I was so excited to see our visitor but oblivious to my parents' dilemma. How would they find gifts when all the stores in town were closed?

Early the next morning, there were stockings and presents under the tree for everyone. I never noticed that Uncle David's gifts looked just like the stuff my Daddy liked.

In the middle of the room sat a child-sized table with, not three, but four little chairs – for me, my two brothers, and Uncle David. I giggled when he scrunched down to sit on his.

Santa truly was magical – he'd brought gifts to our house for Uncle David when no one even knew he was coming.

Or just maybe the magic all along was love – the kind that stretched the presents to go around and made the presence of those we loved the best gift of all.

Dorothy Palmer Young

Beads to inspire:

Love

There is no fear in love; but perfect love casts out fear, because fear involves torment. But he who fears has not been made perfect in love.

(1 John 4:18 NKJV)

Wordwrights OKC Christian Writers
presents:

Erin Taylor Young

Erin Taylor Young is an acquisitions editor for Redbud Press—a boutique publisher focusing on inspirational romance e-books. She loves working with authors but also enjoys working at her local library where she gets to connect readers with books and teach the occasional program about writing and publishing. Between all that, she writes humor. Her recent book, Surviving Henry: Adventures in Loving a Canine Catastrophe, is the story of her noncompliant dog, and has been repeatedly accused of making readers laugh until they cry. Learn more about Erin at www.erintayloryoung.com where she blogs about writing, God, and her aversion to spiders.

A Matter of Trust

Funny how a walk can be the most exciting event of the day for my dog Henry. I mean, right after the excitement of a cookie dropped on the floor.

I pick up his leash and Henry tears through the house, leaping, dancing, and galloping. Yes, he can do all three at once. Then he barrels full tilt toward the door and always realizes a bit too late when it's time to put on the brakes. It goes like this: scramble, scramble…mad dash…hit the wood floor…skiiiiiiiid…face-plant into the six-panel pine.

If I haven't made it to the door by the time he recovers, his excitement turns to desperation, and he launches another antsy-pants dash through the house. Only he runs folded in half, his head skewed around to see if I'm following him, which means he ricochets through the halls like a blind rhinoceros trapped in a breadbox. It's a wonder this dog doesn't knock himself senseless.

When I get to the door, collar and leash in hand, Henry twists, wriggles, and tramps up and down the nearby stairs, because, you know, that makes it so much easier for me to get the collar and leash on him. And of course he whines nonstop through this entire process because I might SOMEHOW forget he wants to go out.

Not that I don't try to carry out this whole procedure with some semblance of decorum. I do. But Henry's not a decorum kind of dog. Still, I won't open the door until he sits calmly. (His version of this means his rump barely touches the floor and his extremities still twitch.)

Heaven help us if he's finally prepped and seated at the door, and I forget something and must walk all of ten feet away to retrieve said item. The dog has a panic attack.

For pity's sake, I'm dressed to take him out, he's wearing the leash, and I'm still looking right at him. Of course we're going for a walk. I'm not abandoning him, I'm just getting my hat.

I wish he could see that. Or at least that he could relax and trust me, even if he doesn't understand my delay.

One day, after months and months of our routine, I have Henry seated precariously at the door when I realize I have yet again forgotten something. My whole body cringes.

"Henry, stay here. I've gotta get a doggie-doo bag."

His eyes flit to me. They're glazed over with one repeating message, "It'swalktimewalktimewalktimewalktime..."

"Yes, I know. And you're sitting very nicely. I just need a bag before we can go."

I take one step and Henry's twitching elevates.

"I'll be right back. I promise."

I could walk him through the house, but it's easier to dig a baggie out of the drawer if I don't have his nose digging through the drawer with me. I head around the corner into the kitchen without him, expecting a panicked Henry at my heels any second.

After a good chunk of rummaging, I turn up the last bag we apparently own. I haven't seen or heard Henry yet, so I hustle back to the door, half worried he keeled over and died.

There he sits, beautifully poised, straight and tall. Alert, but calm. Waiting.

Oh. My. Gosh. He trusts me.

He finally believes I'll follow through on my promise. That I won't bring him to the brink of a goal and then abandon him.

"Henry, I'm so proud of you!" I fawn all over him, giddy not just over his obedience, but over the peace he found in trusting me. It's been a long time coming. A hard time.

Then God's voice nudges my heart. "Henry trusts you, and you delight that he has. So I delight when my children trust me."

The words drop hard in my gut. Oh, how often I've failed in patience, running ahead and slamming into walls. How often I've teetered on the ragged edge of panic, trying to sit still but twitching and whining. How often I've accused God of abandoning his purpose, his promises.

All He wants me to do is trust. Even if He takes longer than I want. Even if it seems God has disappeared from my view.

He isn't gone. He's just putting into motion things that need to happen. Working in ways I can't see or understand any more than Henry can fathom my ways.

I reach for Henry and stroke his fur, filled again with joy for him. At least for today, he's trusting and waiting.

If Henry can do that, so can I. Not only to delight God, but to accept the good he wants for me. Because "blessed is she who has believed that what the Lord has said to her will be accomplished!" (Luke 1:45)

Erin Taylor Young

Beads to inspire:

Peace, Joy, and Love

But the fruit of the Spirit is love, joy, peace, long-suffering, kindness, goodness, faithfulness, gentleness, self-control. Against such there is no law.

(Galatians 5:22,23 NKJV)

Wordwrights OKC Christian Writers
presents:

Barbara Zimmerman

Barbara Zimmerman has written and published two devotionals entitled Paw Prints in my Heart and Paw Prints in my Heart 2 with Mosie Lou. She is currently working on writing a family devotional version of both of the books. She resides in the Oklahoma City area with her cat where she can be contacted at heartwind@barbarazimmerman.com.

Wait 'til Christmas

Do I have to wait 'til Christmas
To celebrate the One
Who walks with me through every day,
Sharing His heart along the way?

Do I have to wait 'til Christmas
To celebrate the One
Who gives Himself continuously
Enabling me to give generously?

Do I have to wait 'til Christmas
To sing of the One
Who alone receives all praise
Being exalted, Ancient of Days?

Do I have to wait 'til Christmas
To look at the One
Who is worthy to be adored
Knowing that He is the Lord of Lords?

I can't, I won't, I choose not to wait;
Jesus! I shall daily celebrate.

Barbara Zimmerman

Thank You for Coming

(A Christmas Prayer)

Thank You for coming into the world
Bringing light for darkness,
peace for war,
love for hatred,
hope for despair.

Thank You for coming into my world
Bringing life to my dead ways,
joy for my sorrows,
peace for my insecurities,
rest for my body and soul.

Thank You for coming such a long time ago –
Love wrapped in flesh
Born to offer change
To the world You created.

Welcome to my world again today.
Please continue bringing
Change my way.

Thank You for coming.

Barbara Zimmerman

BOOKS BY WORDWRIGHTS

To celebrate the 100th birthday of the State of Oklahoma in 2007, members of Wordwrights published the anthology:

A Centennial Celebration of Oklahoma Stories

A few copies of the book's second printing are available through bookstores – Full Circle in Oklahoma City and Best of Books in Edmond, Oklahoma – or via www.barbarashepherd.com

In 2014, members of Wordwrights published a new anthology:

Beads on a String – Peace, Joy, and Love

This book is available in print in bookstores, online, and through several Wordwrights members. Look for it as an e-book on Amazon in 2015.

18471118R00124

Made in the USA
San Bernardino, CA
16 January 2015